I0426419

March 2011

STATE AND LOCAL GOVERNMENTS

Knowledge of Past Recessions Can Inform Future Federal Fiscal Assistance

G A O

Accountability * Integrity * Reliability

STATE AND LOCAL GOVERNMENTS

Knowledge of Past Recessions Can Inform Future Federal Fiscal Assistance

GAO
Accountability • Integrity • Reliability

Highlights

Highlights of GAO-11-401, a report to congressional committees

Why GAO Did This Study

The most recent recession, which started in December 2007, is generally believed to be the worst economic downturn the country has experienced since the Great Depression. In response to this recession, Congress passed the American Recovery and Reinvestment Act of 2009 (Recovery Act), which provided state and local governments with about $282 billion in fiscal assistance. The Recovery Act requires GAO to evaluate how national economic downturns have affected states since 1974. In this report, GAO (1) analyzes how state and local government budgets are affected during national recessions and (2) identifies strategies to provide fiscal assistance to state and local governments and indicators policymakers could use to time and target such assistance. This report is being released in conjunction with a companion report on Medicaid and economic downturns to respond to a related statutory requirement in the Recovery Act. GAO analyzed economic data and states' general fund budget data; reviewed past federal fiscal assistance and related evaluations; and interviewed analysts at key associations and think tanks. GAO shared relevant findings with policy research organizations and associations representing state and local officials, who generally agreed with our conclusions. We incorporated technical comments from the Bureau of Labor Statistics.

GAO identifies strategies for Congress to consider but does not make recommendations in this report.

View GAO-11-401 or key components. For more information, contact Stanley J. Czerwinski at (202) 512-6806 or czerwinskis@gao.gov, or Thomas J. McCool at (202) 512-2700 or mccoolt@gao.gov.

What GAO Found

Understanding state and local government revenue and expenditure patterns can help policymakers determine whether, when, where, and how they provide federal fiscal assistance to state and local governments in response to future national recessions. In general, state and local governments' revenues increase during economic expansions and decline during national recessions (relative to long-run trends). State and local revenue declines have varied during each recession, and the declines have been more severe during recent recessions. Additionally, revenue fluctuations vary substantially across states, due in part to states' differing tax structures, economic conditions, and industrial bases. State and local government spending also tends to increase during economic expansions, but spending on safety net programs, such as health and hospitals and public welfare, appears to decrease during economic expansions and increase during national recessions, relative to long-run trends. These trends can exacerbate the fiscal conditions of state and local governments given that demand for health and other safety net programs increases during recessions, and these programs now consume larger shares of state budgets relative to prior decades. This implies that, during recessions, state and local governments may have difficulties providing services. To mitigate the effect on services from declining revenues, state and local governments take actions including raising taxes and fees, tapping reserves, and using other budget measures to maintain balanced budgets.

Although every recession reflects varied economic circumstances at the national level and among the states, knowledge of prior federal responses to national recessions provides guideposts for policymakers to consider as they design strategies to respond to future recessions. Considerations include

- **Timing** assistance so that the aid begins to flow as the economy is contracting, although assistance that continues for some period beyond the recession's end may help these governments avoid actions that slow economic recovery;
- **Targeting** assistance based on the magnitude of the recession's effects on individual states' economic distress; and
- **Temporarily** increasing federal funding (by specifying the conditions for ending or halting the state and local assistance when states' economic conditions sufficiently improve).

Policymakers also balance their decision to provide state and local assistance with other federal policy considerations such as competing demands for federal resources.

Policymakers can select indicators to identify when the federal government should start and stop providing aid, as well as how much aid should be allocated. Timely indicators are capable of distinguishing states' economic downturns from economic expansions. Indicators selected for targeting assistance are capable of identifying states' individual circumstances in a recession. In general, timely indicators capable of targeting assistance to

_____ **United States Government Accountability Office**

states can be found primarily in labor market data. Indicators such as employment, unemployment, hourly earnings, and wages and salaries also offer the advantage of providing information on economic conditions rather than reflecting states' policy choices (a limitation of data on state revenue trends). In some cases, it may be appropriate for policymakers to select multiple indicators or select indicators to reflect their policy goals specific to a particular recession.

States have been affected differently during each of these recessions. For example, unemployment rates, entry into, and exit out of economic downturns have varied across states during past recessions. Federal responses to prior recessions have included various forms of federal fiscal assistance to these governments as well as decisions not to provide direct fiscal assistance to these governments. In three of the six most recent national recessions, the federal government did not provide fiscal assistance

directly to state and local governments. However, during these recessions, the federal response included increased spending for other programs such as unemployment insurance as well as increases in existing grants not administered by state and local governments. When the federal government has provided fiscal assistance directly to state and local governments in response to national recessions, such assistance has included unrestricted fiscal assistance, increased funding for existing programs, and new grant or loan programs. Federal assistance in response to the recessions beginning in 1973 and 2001 represented a relatively small share of total federal grant funding to the sector. In contrast, the 2009 Recovery Act provided a significant increase in grant funding to the sector and helped offset the sector's tax receipt declines. The figure below summarizes the national unemployment rate, recession dates, and federal fiscal assistance to state and local governments since 1973.

National Unemployment Rate and Federal Fiscal Assistance to State and Local Governments, 1973 to 2010

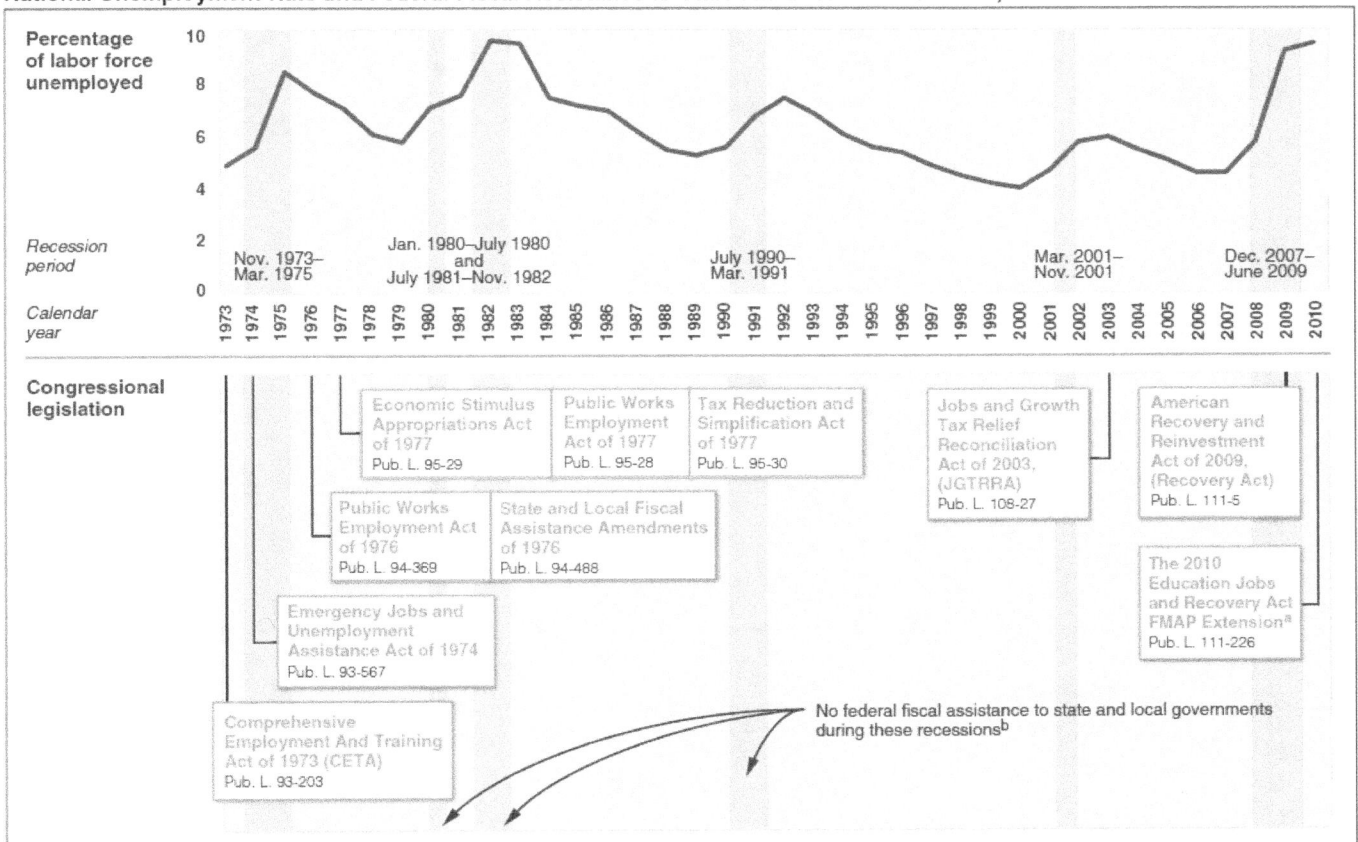

Sources: GAO analysis of BLS and NBER data, federal fiscal assistance public laws, and pertinent legislative history.

[a]Pub. L. No. 111-226 has no official title, so we refer to this act as The 2010 Education Jobs and Recovery Act FMAP Extension.

[b]Other forms of federal assistance were provided, but these approaches did not focus on fiscal assistance to state and local governments.

Contents

Figures

Abbreviations

ARFA	Antirecession Fiscal Assistance
BEA	Bureau of Economic Analysis
BLS	Bureau of Labor Statistics
CES	Current Employment Statistics
CETA	Comprehensive Employment And Training Act of 1973
CBO	Congressional Budget Office
CRS	Congressional Research Service
EECBG	Energy Efficiency and Conservation Block Grant
FMAP	Federal Medical Assistance Percentage
GDI	gross domestic income
GDP	gross domestic product
GSP	gross state product
JGTRRA	Jobs and Growth Tax Relief Reconciliation Act of 2003
LAUS	Local Area Unemployment Statistics
NASBO	National Association of State Budget Officers
NBER	National Bureau of Economic Research
NGA	National Governors Association
NIPA	U.S. National Income and Product Accounts
PCI	per capita income
SAA	State Administering Agency

United States Government Accountability Office
Washington, DC 20548

March 31, 2011

Congressional Committees

The federal government provided fiscal assistance to state and local governments in response to three of the six national recessions since 1974.[1] The most recent recession, which began in December 2007, is generally believed to be the worst economic downturn the country has experienced since the Great Depression. In response to this recession, Congress passed the American Recovery and Reinvestment Act of 2009 (Recovery Act), which provided about $282 billion in federal fiscal assistance to state and local governments.[2] The 2007 recession also brought renewed focus to federal programs that provide fiscal assistance to state governments during economic downturns. We have previously addressed questions about such programs, noting that in providing assistance to state and local governments, it is important to consider the timing, targeting, and amount of assistance based on a variety of factors, including the fiscal health of state governments and the federal government's goals for providing such assistance.[3]

The Recovery Act assigned GAO a range of responsibilities to help promote accountability and transparency as well as to evaluate specific aspects of the act. This report, in conjunction with a companion GAO report on aspects of federal fiscal assistance related to health care, responds to a specific requirement to evaluate how national economic downturns have affected states since 1974—especially with regard to Medicaid—including any recommendations to help address those effects

---

[1]For the purposes of this report, fiscal assistance to state and local governments refers to federal funding provided to state and local governments during economic downturns for the purpose of maintaining or increasing state and local government spending to stimulate macroeconomic activity. Such assistance reduces the likelihood that state and local governments will take contractionary measures, such as increasing taxes or decreasing spending, to stabilize their budgets.

[2]Pub. L. No. 111-5, 123 Stat. 115 (Feb. 17, 2009).

[3]For example, see GAO, *Update of State and Local Government Fiscal Pressures*, GAO-09-320R (Washington, D.C.: Jan. 26, 2009); *Medicaid: Strategies to Help States Address Increased Expenditures during Economic Downturns*, GAO-07-97 (Washington, D.C.: Oct. 18, 2006); and *Federal Assistance: Temporary State Fiscal Relief*, GAO-04-736R (Washington, D.C.: May 07, 2004). See the list of related GAO products included in this report for additional relevant products.

in the future.[4] Accordingly, our objectives for this report are to (1) analyze how state and local government budgets are affected during national recessions and (2) identify what strategies exist to provide federal fiscal assistance to state and local governments during national recessions and indicators policymakers could use to time and target such assistance.

To analyze how national recessions affect state and local governments' revenues, expenditures, and borrowing, we examined data from the Bureau of Economic Analysis's (BEA) National Income and Product Accounts (NIPA), the Census Bureau's Annual Survey of State and Local Government Finances, and the Census Bureau's Census of Governments. To describe state governments' discretionary tax and fee changes and total balances, we collected and analyzed states' general fund data from the National Governors Association (NGA) and National Association of State Budget Officers' (NASBO) *The Fiscal Survey of States* (Fiscal Survey). We assessed the reliability of the data we used for this review and determined that they were sufficiently reliable for our purposes. Appendix I provides additional details about the scope and methodology of our review, including certain limitations concerning the data available for our purposes.

To identify federal strategies for providing federal assistance to state and local governments during national recessions, we reviewed federal fiscal assistance programs enacted since 1973.[5] We identified these programs and potential considerations for designing a federal countercyclical assistance program by reviewing GAO, Congressional Budget Office (CBO), and Congressional Research Service (CRS) reports and conducting a search for relevant legislation. We used these and other reports to identify issues policymakers should consider when selecting a strategy. We also analyzed the legislative history and statutory language of past federal fiscal assistance programs, as well as policy goals stated in the statutes. To identify factors policymakers should consider when selecting indicators to implement their strategy, we reviewed GAO, CBO, CRS, Federal Reserve Banks, Department of the Treasury (Treasury), and academic reports. We considered indicators' availability at the state level and timeliness (in terms of frequency and publication lag time) to identify

---

[4]GAO, *Medicaid: Improving Responsiveness of Federal Assistance to States during Economic Downturns*, GAO-11-395 (Washington, D.C.: March 31, 2011).

[5]Although GAO's mandate refers to national economic downturns since 1974, we extended our review to 1973 to capture the recession that began in November 1973.

indicators policymakers could use to time and target federal fiscal assistance during national recessions.[6] Finally, we interviewed key associations and think tanks familiar with the design and implementation of programs providing federal fiscal assistance to state and local governments to understand the range of perspectives regarding these programs and to identify relevant related research on these issues.

We provided relevant sections of a draft of this report to the Bureau of Labor Statistics and external experts. They offered technical suggestions, which we incorporated as appropriate.

We conducted this performance audit from February 2010 to March 2011, in accordance with generally accepted government auditing standards. Those standards require that we plan and perform the audit to obtain sufficient, appropriate evidence to provide a reasonable basis for our findings and conclusions based on our audit objectives. We believe that the evidence obtained provides a reasonable basis for our findings and conclusions based on our audit objectives.

Background

Recessions mark a distinct phase of the overall business cycle, beginning with a business cycle "peak" and ending with a business cycle "trough." Between trough and peak the economy is in an expansion. The National Bureau of Economic Research (NBER) identifies dates for national recessions, which can vary in overall duration and magnitude.[7] While NBER sets dates for the peaks and troughs of national recessions, no dates are set for turning points in state economies. State economic downturns vary in magnitude, duration, and timing, and do not necessarily coincide with dates identified for national recessions.

---

[6]We refer to national recessions throughout this report to distinguish recessions declared by the National Bureau of Economic Research (NBER) from state-level economic downturns. We use the term "national recession" to refer to the period between the business cycle peak and trough dates identified by NBER. We use the term "economic downturn" to refer more generally to reductions in output, income, and employment that occur at either the state or national level. Every national recession is a national economic downturn, but not every national economic downturn is a national recession. Similarly, state-level downturns in economic activity do not necessarily correspond with periods of national recession identified by NBER.

[7]The NBER is a private, nonprofit, nonpartisan research organization dedicated to promoting a greater understanding of how the economy works.

Characteristics of National Recessions

NBER defines a recession as a significant decline in economic activity spread across the economy, lasting more than a few months, normally visible in real gross domestic product (GDP), real income, employment, industrial production, and wholesale-retail sales. NBER uses several monthly indicators to identify national recessions. These indicators include measures of GDP and gross domestic income (GDI), real personal income excluding transfers, the payroll and household measures of total employment, and aggregate hours of work in the total economy.[8]

Since 1973, NBER has identified six national recessions. These recessions have varied considerably in duration and magnitude (table 1). For example, real GDP declined by 4.1 percent over the course of the 2007-2009 recession, which lasted 18 months. Similarly, real GDP declined by about 3 percent during the 1973-1975 and 1981-1982 recessions, both of which lasted 16 months. In contrast, real GDP declined 1.4 percent and 0.7 percent in the 1990 and 2001 recessions, respectively, both of which lasted 8 months.

Table 1: Variations in U.S. National Recessions, 1973 to Present

Recession period	Recession duration (in months)	Maximum unemployment rate (in percent)	Measure of magnitude (Percentage change from peak to trough)				
			Real GDP	Real private consumption	Real personal income less transfers	Payroll survey employment	Household survey employment
Nov. 1973 to Mar. 1975	16	8.6	-3.2	-0.8	-5.3	-1.6	-1.3
Jan. 1980 to July 1980	6	7.8	-2.2	-1.2	-2.3	-1.1	-1.1
July 1981 to Nov. 1982	16	10.8	-2.6	2.9	-0.1	-3.1	-1.6
July 1990 to Mar. 1991	8	6.8	-1.4	-1.1	-2.1	-1.1	-1.0
Mar. 2001 to Nov. 2001	8	5.5	0.7	2.4	-1.2	-1.2	-1.1
Dec. 2007 to June 2009	18	9.5	-4.1	-2.4	-5.6	-5.4	-4.3

Source: GAO analysis of BEA, BLS, and NBER data.

[8]The NBER dating committee weighs the behavior of various indicators because economic indicators do not typically move exactly in concert. For example, aggregate hours and employment have frequently reached their troughs at later dates than NBER's trough date in previous business cycles. In the 2007 recession, employment levels reached their trough 6 months after the NBER trough.

Notes: A trough occurs when the declining phase of the business cycle ends and the rising phase of the business cycle begins. Similar economic patterns may not repeat themselves in future economic downturns.

Characteristics of State Economic Downturns

States are affected differently by national recessions. For example, unemployment rates have varied across states during past recessions.[9] During the course of the 2007-2009 recession, the national unemployment rate nearly doubled, increasing from 5.0 percent to 9.5 percent. The unemployment rate in individual states increased between 1.4 and 6.8 percentage points, with a median change of 4 percentage points (figure 1). In contrast, a smaller national unemployment rate increase of 1.3 percentage points during the 1990-1991 recession reflected unemployment rate changes in individual states ranging from -0.2 to 3.4 percentage points.

---

[9]The unemployment rate represents the number unemployed as a percent of the labor force. People who are jobless, looking for jobs, and available for work are unemployed. People who do not have a job and are not looking for one are not considered part of the labor force.

Figure 1: Variation in Percentage Point Changes in State Unemployment Rates during Past National Recessions

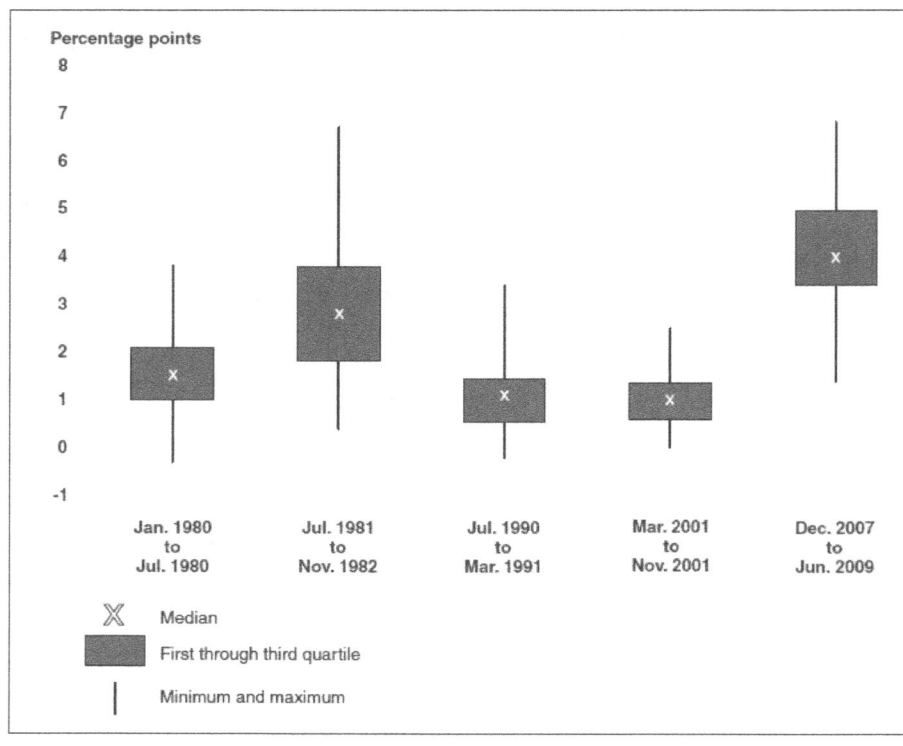

Source: GAO analysis of BLS data.

Note: The figure depicts percentage point changes in unemployment rather than actual unemployment rates. We calculated the change in unemployment by subtracting each state's unemployment rate at the time of an NBER trough from the unemployment rate at an NBER peak. The 1973 recession is excluded because the BLS data series used begins with 1976.

Recent economic research suggests that while economic downturns within states generally occur around the same time as national recessions, their timing—or entrance into and exit out of the economic downturn— and duration varies.[10] Some states may enter or exit an economic

---

[10]For example, see Michael T. Owyang, Jeremy Piger, and Howard J. Wall, "Business Cycle Phases in U.S. States," *The Review of Economics and Statistics* 87(4) (November 2005): 604-616 and Theodore M. Crone, "What a New Set of Indexes Tells Us About State and National Business Cycles," *The Federal Reserve Bank of Philadelphia Business Review* (Q1 2006):11-24.

downturn before or after a national recession. Other states' economies may expand while the country as a whole is in recession. States can also experience an economic downturn not associated with a national recession. States' differing characteristics, such as industrial structure, contribute to these differences in economic activity. For example, manufacturing states tend to experience economic downturns sooner than other states in a recession, while energy sector states are often out of sync with the country as a whole.

Federal Actions in Response to National Recessions

The federal government has multiple policy options at its disposal for responding to national recessions, although federal policy responses are not necessarily limited to the time periods of national recession.[11] For example, in response to the recession beginning in December 2007, the federal government and the Federal Reserve together acted to moderate the downturn and restore economic growth when confronted with unprecedented weakness in the financial sector and the overall economy. The Federal Reserve used monetary policy to respond to the recession by pursuing one of the most significant interest rate reductions in U.S. history. In concert with the Department of the Treasury, it went on to bolster the supply of credit in the economy through measures that provide Federal Reserve backing for a wide variety of loan types, from mortgages to automobile loans to small business loans.

The federal government also used fiscal policy to confront the effects of the recession. Existing fiscal stabilizers, such as unemployment insurance and progressive aspects of the tax code, kicked in automatically in order to ease the pressure on household income as economic conditions deteriorated. In addition, Congress enacted legislation providing temporary tax cuts for businesses and a tax rebate for individuals in the first half of 2008 to buoy incomes and spending[12] and created the Troubled

---

[11]For an overview of other policy options for responding to national recessions, see Congressional Budget Office, *Policies for Increasing Economic Growth and Employment in 2010 and 2011* (Washington, D.C.: Jan. 2010); and Congressional Budget Office, *The State of the Economy and Issues in Developing an Effective Policy Response*, Statement of Douglas W. Elmendorf before the Committee on the Budget, U.S. House of Representatives (Washington, D.C.: Jan. 27, 2009).

[12]Economic Stimulus Act of 2008, Pub. L. No. 110-185, 122 Stat. 613 (Feb. 13, 2008).

GAO-11-401 State and Local Governments

Asset Relief Program[13] in the second half of 2008 to give Treasury authority to act to restore financial market functioning.[14]

The federal government's largest response to the recession to date came in early 2009 with the passage of the Recovery Act, the broad purpose of which is to stimulate the economy's overall demand for goods and services, or aggregate demand. Fiscal stimulus programs are intended to increase aggregate demand—the spending of consumers, business firms, and governments—and may be either automatic or discretionary. Unemployment insurance, the progressive aspects of the tax code, and other fiscal stabilizers provide stimulus automatically by easing pressure on household incomes as economic conditions deteriorate. Discretionary fiscal stimulus, such as that provided by the Recovery Act, can take the form of tax cuts for households and businesses, transfers to individuals, grants-in-aid to state and local governments, or direct federal spending. In response, households, businesses, and governments may purchase more goods and services than they would have otherwise, and governments and businesses may refrain from planned workforce cuts or even hire additional workers. Thus, fiscal stimulus may lead to an overall, net increase in national employment and output.

The federal government may have an interest in providing fiscal assistance to state and local governments during recessions because doing so could reduce actions taken by these governments that could exacerbate the effects of the recession. Output, income, and employment all tend to fall during recessions, causing state and local governments to collect less revenue at the same time that demand for the goods and services they provide is increasing. Since state governments typically face balanced budget requirements and other constraints, they adjust to this situation by raising taxes, cutting programs and services, or drawing down reserve funds, all but the last of which amplify short-term recessionary pressure

---

[13]GAO, *Troubled Asset Relief Program: One Year Later, Actions Are Needed to Address Remaining Transparency and Accountability Challenges*, GAO-10-16 (Washington, D.C.: Oct. 8, 2009).

[14]Emergency Economic Stabilization Act of 2008, Pub. L. No. 110-343, 122 Stat. 3765 (Oct. 3, 2008), codified at 12 U.S.C. §§ 5201-5261.

on households and businesses.[15] Local governments may make similar adjustments unless they can borrow to make up for reduced revenue. By providing assistance to state and local governments, the federal government may be able to forestall, or at least moderate, state and local governments' program and service cuts, tax increases, and liquidation of reserves. The federal government has provided varied forms of assistance directly to state and local governments in response to three of the past six recessions (figure 2).[16] States have been affected differently during each of these recessions. For example, unemployment rates, entry into, and exit out of economic downturns have varied across states during past recessions. See appendix III for a description of each piece of legislation.

---

[15]According to the National Association of State Budget Officers (NASBO), most states have balanced-budget requirements for general funds, which may include requirements such as (1) requiring governors to submit a balanced budget, (2) mandating that their legislatures pass a balanced budget, (3) directing governors to sign a balanced budget, or (4) requiring governors to execute a balanced budget. Although most states have balanced budget requirements, these requirements typically apply to enacted budgets or to the governors' proposed budgets. See NASBO, *Budget Processes in the States* (Washington, D.C.: Summer 2008).

[16]However, during the three recessions where the federal government did not provide fiscal assistance, the federal response included increased spending for other programs such as unemployment insurance as well as increases in existing grants not administered by state and local governments.

GAO-11-401 State and Local Governments

Figure 2: National Unemployment Rate and Federal Fiscal Assistance to State and Local Governments, 1973 to 2010

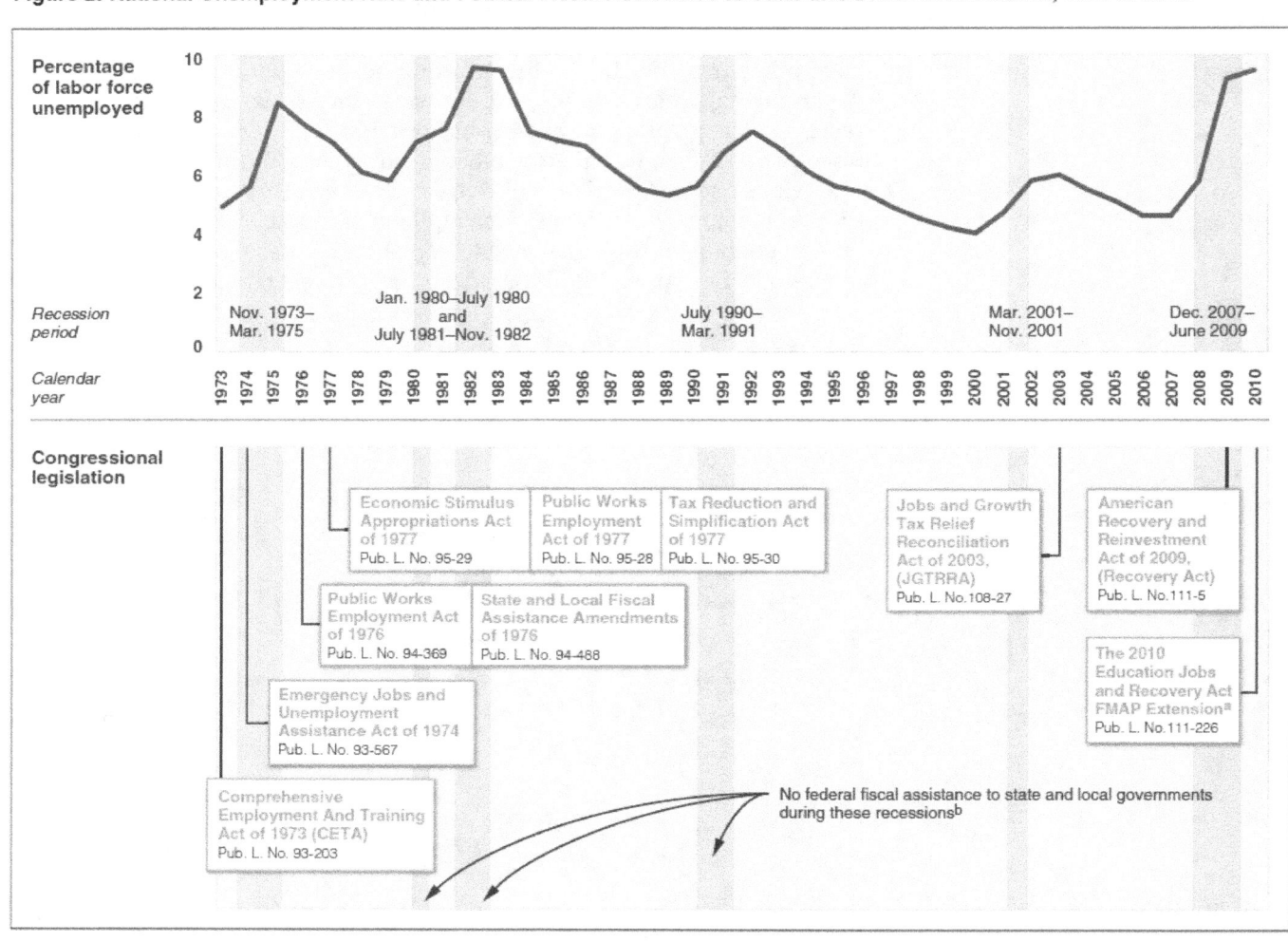

Sources: GAO analysis of BLS and NBER data, federal fiscal assistance public laws, and pertinent legislative history.

[a]Pub. L. No. 111-226 has no official title, so we refer to this act as The 2010 Education Jobs and Recovery Act FMAP Extension.

[b]Other forms of federal assistance were provided, but these approaches did not focus on fiscal assistance to state and local governments. These other forms of federal assistance included: The Job Training Partnership Act, Pub. L. No. 97-300 (Oct. 13, 1982); Public Law No. 98-8, known as the Emergency Jobs Appropriations Act of 1983 (March 24, 1983); and the Supplemental Appropriations Act of 1993, Pub. L. No. 103-50 (July 2, 1993).

Congressional decisions about whether to provide fiscal assistance to state and local governments ultimately depend on what role policymakers believe the federal government should take during future national recessions. Perspectives on whether and the extent to which the federal government should provide fiscal assistance to state and local governments are far-ranging—some advocate for not creating an expectation that federal fiscal assistance will be provided, while others argue for a greater federal role in providing fiscal assistance to state and local governments in response to national recessions.

Some policy analysts warn against creating an expectation that federal assistance will be available to state and local governments.[17] These analysts contend that federal fiscal assistance can distort state and local fiscal choices and induce greater spending of scarce state funds. For example, the matching requirements of federal grants can induce state governments to dedicate more resources than they otherwise would to areas where these resources are not necessarily required. According to these analysts, federal fiscal assistance to state and local governments reduces government accountability and erodes state control by imposing federal solutions on state problems. Those who hold this perspective see little justification for insulating state governments from the same fiscal discipline that other sectors of the economy follow during a recession.

In contrast, other policy analysts favor a federal role in promoting the fiscal health of state and local governments during economic downturns.[18] Proponents of this view contend that during economic downturns, state and local governments face the dilemma that demand for social welfare benefits increases at the same time that state and local governments' ability to meet these demands is constrained as a result of decreasing tax revenues.

---

[17]For example, see GAO-04-736R; Advisory Commission on Intergovernmental Relations, *Countercyclical Aid and Economic Stabilization*, A-69 (Washington D.C.: December 1978); and Eileen Norcross and Frederic Sautet, "The American Recovery and Reinvestment Act: Is More Federal Grant Money What the States Need?" *Mercatus on Policy*, No. 36 (Washington, D.C.: Mercatus Center, January 2009).

[18]For example, see Sherle R. Schwenninger, *The American Social Contract: Lessons from the Great Recession*, (Washington, D.C.: The New America Foundation, September 2010); Scott Lilly, *Pumping Life Back into the U.S. Economy: Why a Stimulus Package Must Be Big and Targeted* (Washington, D.C.: Center for American Progress, January 2009); Max Sawicky, "An Idea Whose Time has Returned: Anti-recession Fiscal Assistance for State and Local Governments," *Briefing Paper* (Washington, D.C.: Economic Policy Institute, October 2001).

State and Local Governments' Revenue and Expenditure Patterns during National Recessions Reflect Variations in Economic Circumstances and Policy Choices

State and Local Government Revenue Declines in National Recessions Vary in Magnitude, over Time, and across States

General revenues collected by state and local governments over the past three decades are procyclical—typically increasing when the national economy is expanding and decreasing during national recessions, relative to their long-run trend.[19] Own-source revenues, which made up about 80 percent of state and local general revenues in 2008, and total tax revenues, which made up about 68 percent of state and local own-source revenues in 2008, display similar cyclical behavior. In addition, state and local revenue growth lagged the resumption of national economic growth after the 2001

---

[19]General revenues comprise all revenue except that classified as liquor store, utility, or insurance trust revenue. General revenues collected by the state and local government sector in the United States are either collected from own-sources or are intergovernmental revenues received from the federal government. To describe how state and local government revenues change during national economic downturns, we used data from the Annual Survey of State and Local Government Finances and Census of Governments collected by the U.S. Census Bureau, as well as data from the National Income and Product Accounts produced by the Bureau of Economic Analysis. We analyzed data for the United States for the period 1977-2008. We first decomposed real state and local government revenues and GDP into their (1) long-run trend and (2) business cycle components. We then calculated the correlations of the business cycle components of state and local government revenues with the business cycle component of GDP. The cyclical components of revenues and of GDP are the percent deviations in revenues and GDP from their long-run trends. In general, a positive correlation indicates that revenues are procyclical and a negative correlation indicates that revenues are countercyclical. Specifically, we identified revenues as procyclical if the correlation was greater than or equal to 0.2, and we identified revenues as countercyclical if the correlation was less than or equal to -0.2. Appendix I contains additional details on our methodology and its limitations, and appendix II contains definitions of state and local government revenues.

and 2007-2009 recessions, but preceded it during the 1981-1982 and 1990-1991 recessions.

State and local governments' current tax receipts have declined in each of the six national recessions since 1973. However, both the severity of these revenue declines and the time it has taken for revenues to recover has varied (figure 3).[20] During the most recent recession, state and local governments experienced more severe and long-lasting declines in revenue than in past recessions. For example, over the course of the 2007-2009 recession, current tax receipts declined 9.2 percent—from $1.4 trillion in the fourth quarter of 2007 to $1.2 trillion in the second quarter of 2009—and had not yet returned to the peak level 5 quarters after the end of the recession. In contrast, the recessions beginning in 1980, 1981, and 1990 were less severe. For example, over the course of the 1990-1991 recession, current tax receipts declined less than 1 percent—from $789 billion in the third quarter of 1990 to about $785 billion in the first quarter of 1991—and recovered as the recession ended in the first quarter of 1991.

[20]In our analysis of the magnitude of revenue declines during national recessions, we used state and local government tax receipt data from the Bureau of Economic Analysis for the first quarter of 1973 to the third quarter of 2010. Unless otherwise stated, current tax receipts are presented in real 2009 dollars.

Figure 3: Changes in State and Local Government Current Tax Receipts during National Recessions, 1973 through 2010

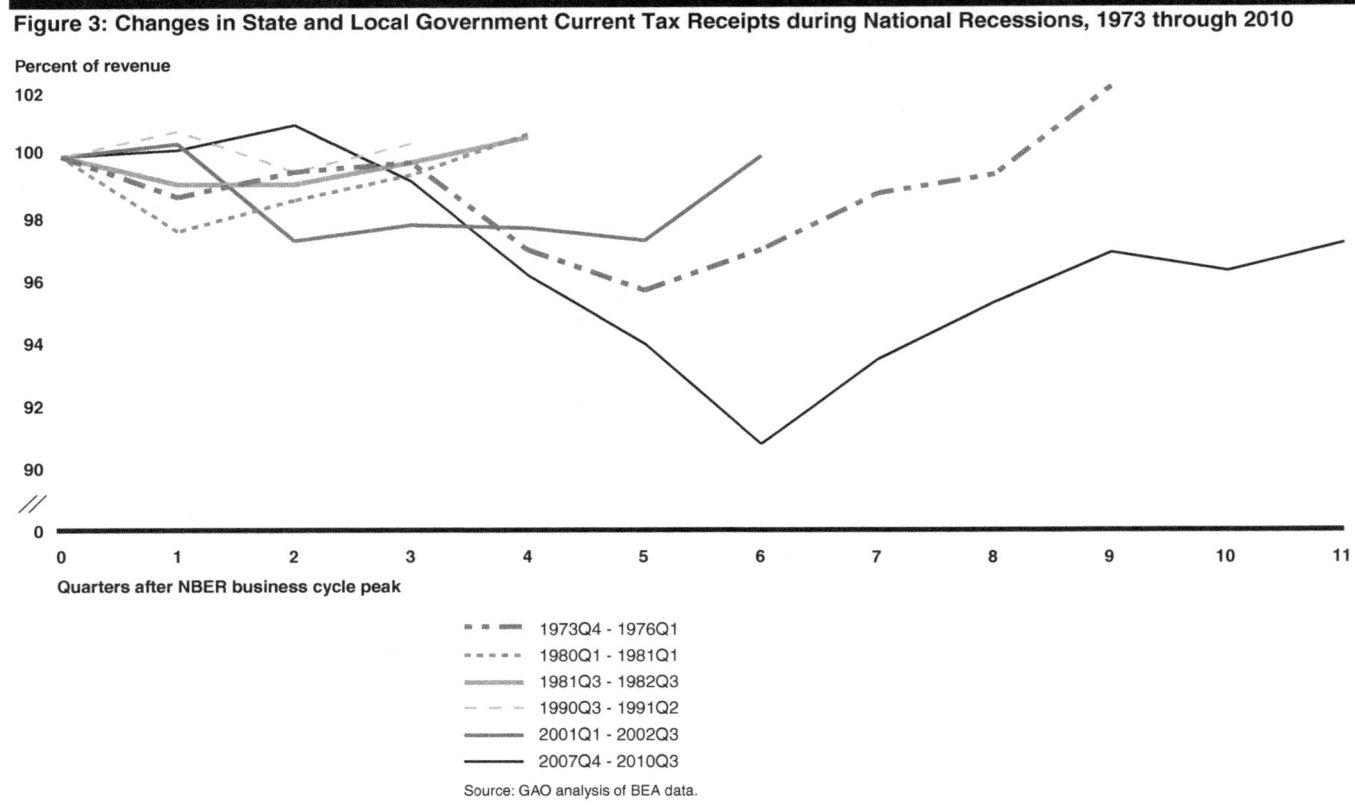

Percent of revenue

Quarters after NBER business cycle peak

— — — 1973Q4 - 1976Q1
- - - - - 1980Q1 - 1981Q1
———— 1981Q3 - 1982Q3
– – – 1990Q3 - 1991Q2
———— 2001Q1 - 2002Q3
———— 2007Q4 - 2010Q3

Source: GAO analysis of BEA data.

Note: Quarter 0 denotes the peak of an NBER business cycle. The number of quarters shown for each recession represents the amount of time needed for tax receipts to return to or surpass their levels at the beginning of the recession period (NBER business cycle peak). For the 2007 recession, receipts have yet to return to their peak levels. The levels of state and local current tax receipts for each recession are indexed to their levels at the beginning of the recession period. Current tax receipts are tax revenues received by these governments from all sources.

Larger revenue declines during the two most recent recessions have coincided with increased volatility in state and local government revenues during the past two decades. This increased volatility can be attributed to the fact that since 1973, states have become increasingly reliant on individual income taxes, which are usually more volatile than other revenues.[21] Income tax receipts rose from 15 percent of current tax

---

[21]While it is not always clear which type of tax is most volatile, state governments that diversify their tax bases may see less volatility in their tax receipts than those that are more heavily dependent on fewer types of taxes.

GAO-11-401 State and Local Governments

receipts in 1973 to 20 percent in 2009. Analysts have attributed the increase in income tax as a portion of state revenues to state policy changes favoring income taxes and changes in the ways workers are compensated.[22] Over time, state and local government revenues have become more volatile due to an increased reliance on income tax and a decreased reliance on sales tax. Several factors have contributed to these shifts, including sales tax exemptions for certain items, such as food and medicine; an increase in the share of consumption represented by services, as services are often excluded from sales tax; and increased Internet sales, which can reduce opportunities for state tax collections.

Revenue fluctuations during national recessions vary substantially across states. Analysts have reported that this is due in part to states' differing tax structures, economic conditions, and industrial bases. The aggregate revenue levels described earlier mask varying trends among individual state and local governments, as some state and local governments experience minimal or no revenue declines during national recessions, while others face severe reductions in tax revenues. For example, the median decline in state tax collections from the first quarter of 2008 to the first quarter of 2009 was 11 percent. While variations ranged from a 72 percent decline to a 15 percent increase during this period, most individual state tax collections declined between 16 percent and 6 percent.

To better understand the extent to which an individual state's government tax revenues decline during national recessions, we estimated how responsive state government tax revenues are to changes in total wages, a proxy for the amount of economic activity.[23] We found that, on average, state tax revenues decrease by 1 percent when wages decrease by about 1 percent. However, this effect varies substantially across individual states, with state tax revenues falling by anywhere from about 0.2 percent to about 1.8 percent in response to a 1 percent decline in wages. This means

[22]Analysts have reported that capital gains income rose absolutely and as a share of individual income during the 1990s. Factors contributing to this trend include individuals generating taxable income by (1) selling financial assets as stock and bond prices rose and (2) exercising stock options, which had become a more common form of employee compensation. For example, see Tim Schiller, "Riding the Revenue Roller Coaster: Recent Trends in State Government Finance," *Federal Reserve Bank of Philadelphia Business Review*, Q1/2010.

[23]This analysis covered the second quarter of 1992 through the first quarter of 2010. Data on total state tax revenues are from the U.S. Census Bureau's Quarterly Summary of State and Local Government Tax Revenue. State wage data are from the U.S. Bureau of Labor Statistics' Quarterly Census of Employment and Wages.

that given the same reduction in wages, one state's tax revenues may fall at up to nine times the rate of another state.

State and Local Government Spending Increases during Economic Expansions and Decreases during National Recessions Relative to Long-Run Trends While Spending on Safety Net Programs Displays the Opposite Pattern

General expenditures by state and local governments are procyclical (table 2).[24] General expenditures also tend to lag the national business cycle by one to two years, so they tend to decline relative to trend later than GDP and also to increase relative to trend later than GDP. However, general expenditures by state and local governments grew at an average annual rate of about 4 percent during the period from 1977 to 2008, so declines in general expenditures relative to trend do not necessarily correspond to absolute declines in the level of general expenditures.[25]

Table 2: Cyclical Behavior of State and Local Government Expenditures, 1977 to 2008

Expenditure function	Correlation with GDP	Cyclical behavior
General expenditures	0.34	Procyclical
Capital outlays	0.50	Procyclical
Current expenditures	0.23	Procyclical
Elementary and secondary education	0.60	Procyclical
Higher education	0.29	Procyclical
Health and hospitals	-0.36	Countercyclical
Highways	0.53	Procyclical
Police and corrections	0.38	Procyclical
Public welfare	-0.31	Countercyclical
All other current expenditures	0.40	Procyclical

Source: GAO analysis of BEA and U.S. Census Bureau data.

[24]Our analysis of state and local government expenditures used data from the Annual Surveys of State and Local Government Finances and the Census of Governments collected by the U.S. Census Bureau, which were available for the years 1977 to 2008, as well as data from the National Income and Product Accounts produced by the Bureau of Economic Analysis for the same time period. General expenditures include all expenditures except those classified as utility, liquor store, or social insurance trust expenditures. See appendix I for a description of our methodology and its limitations. See appendix II for a description of state and local government expenditures.

[25]If spending is growing, but growing at a rate that is slower than its long-term trend growth rate, then spending is declining relative to trend, even though the absolute level of spending is increasing.

Notes: To describe how state and local government expenditures change during national economic downturns, we first decomposed real state and local government expenditures and GDP into their (1) long-run trend and (2) business cycle components. We then calculated the correlations of the business cycle components of state and local government expenditures with the business cycle component of GDP. We used data for the period 1977 to 2008 for the United States. The cyclical components of expenditures and of GDP are the percent deviations in expenditures and GDP from their long-run trends. In general, a positive correlation indicates that expenditures are procyclical and a negative correlation indicates that expenditures are countercyclical. Specifically, we identified revenues as procyclical if the correlation was greater than or equal to 0.2, and we identified revenues as countercyclical if the correlation was less than or equal to -0.2. Our results may be sensitive to the method we used to estimate the business cycle components of expenditures and of GDP, may not generalize to other time periods, and may not apply to individual U.S. states. Appendix I contains additional details on our methodology and its limitations. Appendix II contains definitions of state and local government expenditures.

Both of the main components of general expenditures—capital outlays and current expenditures—are procyclical. Capital outlays, which made up about 13 percent of general expenditures in 2008, are expenditures on the purchase of buildings, land, and equipment, among other things. Current expenditures, which made up the remaining 87 percent of general expenditures in 2008, include all non-investment spending, such as supplies, materials, and contractual services for current operations; wages and salaries for employees; and cash assistance to needy individuals. Capital outlays show a stronger procyclical relationship than current expenditures, and therefore typically fall relative to trend more than current expenditures during national recessions. Trends in capital outlays and current expenditures tend to lag the national business cycle by 1 to 2 years. However, like general expenditures, both capital outlays and current expenditures by state and local government grew by approximately 4 percent per year between 1977 and 2008, so declines below their long-run trends do not imply that the levels of either capital outlays or current expenditures declined.

Spending associated with social safety net programs appears to behave differently over the business cycle than other types of spending. For example, current expenditures on health and hospitals and on public welfare–expenditures associated with social safety net programs such as Medicaid and Temporary Assistance for Needy Families (TANF)— typically increase relative to trend during national recessions (i.e., these expenditures are countercyclical).[26] In contrast, current expenditures on

---

[26]Similarly, current expenditures on health and hospitals and on public welfare typically decrease relative to trend during national economic expansions. Spending on health and hospitals and public welfare now consume larger shares of state budgets relative to prior decades. See GAO, *State and Local Governments: Fiscal Pressures Could Have Implications for Future Delivery of Intergovernmental Programs*, GAO-10-899 (Washington, D.C.: July 30, 2010).

elementary and secondary education, higher education, highways, and police and corrections typically decrease relative to trend during economic downturns (i.e., these expenditures are procyclical). Current expenditures on health and hospitals and on public welfare may be countercyclical because the number of people living in poverty is one of the main drivers of both types of expenditures, and the number of people living in poverty tends to increase during national recessions and to decrease during national expansions.

In addition, current expenditures on some functions seem to lag the business cycle more than others. For example, current expenditures on elementary and secondary education and higher education seem to lag the business cycle by 1 to 2 years, while current expenditures on other functions do not seem to lag the business cycle. Thus, while state and local governments tend to reduce total current expenditures relative to trend during national recessions, they do not do so for every service. Furthermore, current expenditures on some services, such as education, take longer to recover than others after the recession is over. However, current expenditures on all the services we analyzed grew every year on average during the period of 1977 to 2008, so declines relative to trend were not necessarily absolute declines in spending on these services.

If state and local government expenditures are typically procyclical, then state and local governments may have difficulties providing services during recessions. Reduced expenditures relative to trend during recessions may be reflecting reduced revenues relative to trend rather than reduced desire for services. For example, current expenditures on elementary and secondary education tend to fall relative to trend during recessions, but the population of elementary and secondary school-age children is unlikely to vary much as a result of the business cycle. Current expenditures on higher education also tend to fall relative to trend during recessions even though enrollment in colleges and universities may increase during recessions.[27] Furthermore, the finding that current expenditures on health and hospitals and on public welfare tend to

---

[27]For example, researchers have found that as unemployment increases during a recession, unemployed individuals may return to school to obtain additional skills, certifications, or degrees. See Julian R. Betts and Laurel L. McFarland, "Safe Port in a Storm: The Impact of Labor Market Conditions on Community College Enrollments," *Journal of Human Resources* 30(4), Autumn 1995, 741-765; Harris Dellas and Vally Koubi, "Business Cycles and Schooling," *European Journal of Political Economy* 19 (2003), 843-859; and Harris Dellas and Plutarchos Sakellaris, "On the Cyclicality of Schooling: Theory and Evidence," *Oxford Economic Papers* 55, January 2003, 148-172.

increase relative to trend during recessions does not definitively indicate the extent to which these increases are meeting increased demand during recessions. For example, we have previously reported that economic downturns in states result in rising unemployment, which can lead to increases in the number of individuals who are eligible for Medicaid coverage, and in declining tax revenues, which can lead to less available revenue with which to fund coverage of additional enrollees. Between 2001 and 2002, Medicaid enrollment rose 8.6 percent, which was largely attributed to states' increases in unemployment. During this same period, state tax revenues fell 7.5 percent.[28] The extent to which state governments maintained the capacity to fund their Medicaid programs differed during past recessions. These differences reflect variations in state unemployment rate increases and varied increases in Medicaid enrollment during recession periods.[29]

State Governments Raise Taxes and Fees, Tap Reserves, and Use Other Budget Measures to Address Revenue Declines during National Recessions

As revenues decline and demand increases for programs such as Medicaid and unemployment insurance during national recessions, state governments make fiscal choices within the constraints of their available resources. These decisions typically entail raising taxes, tapping reserves, reducing spending (as described earlier), or using other budget strategies to respond to revenue declines.

[28]GAO-07-97.

[29]GAO-11-395 provides additional information regarding these variations.

State Governments Increase Taxes and Fees to Respond to Revenue Shortfalls during National Recessions, but Individual State Policy Choices Vary

In our analysis of the discretionary changes state governments have made to their revenue policies since 1990, we found that—in the aggregate— state governments made policy changes to increase taxes and fees during or after every national recession since state fiscal year 1990 (figure 4).[30] For example, tax and fee increases as a percent of state general fund revenue peaked at about 5.1 percent in state fiscal year 1992, about 1.8 percent in state fiscal year 2004, and about 3.9 percent in state fiscal year 2010. From state fiscal years 1995 to 2001, states reduced taxes and fees by amounts ranging from 0.7 percent to 1.5 percent of general fund revenues. From state fiscal years 2003 to 2008, discretionary changes in states' taxes and fees ranged from -0.3 percent to 1.8 percent.[31]

---

[30]For all descriptions of policy changes in this section, we analyzed aggregate changes in state policy choices by calculating the net sum of the tax and fee increases and decreases that states enacted during each fiscal year, and dividing the result by states' total general fund revenues. Calculations are based on figures presented in NGA and NASBO's *The Fiscal Survey of States*. We limited our review to state fiscal years 1990 to 2010 because these are the years data on enacted revenue changes are available in NGA and NASBO's *The Fiscal Survey of States*. The federal fiscal year begins on October 1 and ends on September 30. In contrast, state fiscal years begin on July 1 and end on June 30 for all but four states (Alabama, Michigan, New York, and Texas). We limited our review to state revenue actions, as NASBO has only included information on state program area cuts in its last four Fiscal Surveys.

[31]It remains to be seen whether the aftermath of the 2007 recession will follow the same path to state and local government revenue recovery as prior recessions. Projections for continued unemployment rates of 9 percent or more through 2011 and constrained GDP growth for the next several years result in uncertainty regarding the number of years until revenues return to 2007 levels.

GAO-11-401 State and Local Governments

Figure 4: State Government Aggregate Tax and Fee Policy Changes as a Percentage of General Fund Revenues, State Fiscal Years 1990 to 2010

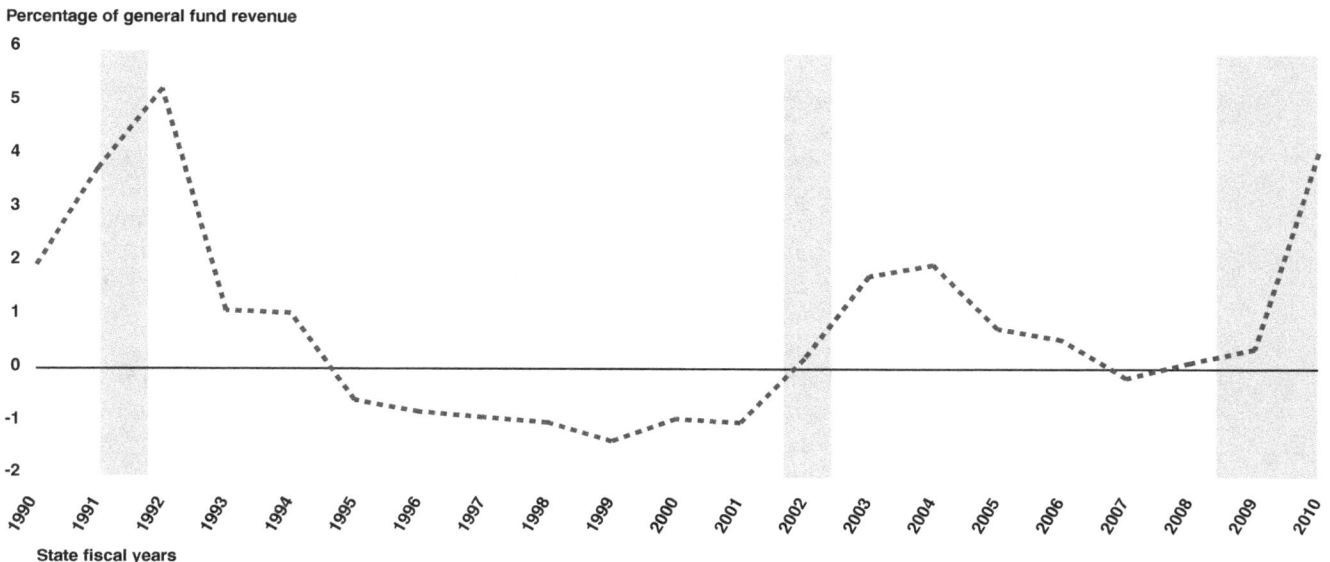

NBER recessions

• • • • • States' tax and fee policy changes

Source: GAO analysis of data from NGA, NASBO, and NBER.

Notes: Data for state fiscal year 2010 are estimated based on general fund amounts reported by state budget offices. NASBO conducted its 2010 survey from March through May 2010 and reported amounts reflect enacted budget actions. Reported amounts do not include all states in all years. NBER recession dates are reported in state fiscal years, which begin on July 1 of each calendar year for all but four states (Alabama, Michigan, New York, and Texas). For example, we illustrate the national recession beginning July 1990 and ending March 1991 as beginning in the first month of state fiscal year 1991 and ending the ninth month of state fiscal year 1991.

Within these national trends, individual state revenue policy choices varied considerably during our period of analysis. For example, in state fiscal year 1992, state governments enacted changes equal to 5.1 percent of general fund revenues for all states in the aggregate. However, during that fiscal year, individual states' policy changes ranged from reducing taxes and fees by 1.4 percent to raising taxes and fees by 21.3 percent of general fund revenues. In state fiscal year 2008, aggregate state policy changes were about 0 percent of general fund revenues, but individual state policy changes ranged from decreasing taxes and fees by 6.1 percent to increasing taxes and fees by 19.3 percent.

GAO-11-401 State and Local Governments

State Governments Tap Fiscal Reserves to Address Declines in Revenue During and After Periods of National Recession

As we have previously reported, most state governments prepare for future budget uncertainty by establishing fiscal reserves.[32] NASBO has reported that 48 states have budget stabilization funds, which may be budget reserves, revenue-shortfall accounts, or cash-flow accounts.[33]

State governments have tapped fiscal reserves to cope with revenue shortfalls during recent national recessions, as indicated by their reported total balances, which are comprised of general fund ending balances and the amounts in state budget stabilization "rainy day" funds (figure 5).[34] Prior to the recessions beginning in 2000 and 2007, state governments built large balance levels, in the aggregate. According to NGA and NASBO's *Fiscal Survey of States*, these balance levels reached 10.4 percent of expenditures in state fiscal year 2000 and 11.5 percent in 2006. Total balances typically reached their lowest points during or just after national recessions. By state fiscal year 2003, states' total balances dropped to 3.2 percent of expenditures, and in fiscal year 2010 they had fallen to 6.4 percent. These total balance levels appear inflated, however, because individual state governments' reserves can vary substantially. For example, NASBO reports that for state fiscal year 2010, two states (Texas and Alaska) represented $25.4 billion—more than 64 percent—of all state governments' total balances. Removing these states, total balances were 2.4 percent of expenditures for the remaining 48 state governments.

---

[32]GAO, *Budgeting for Emergencies: State Practices and Federal Implications*, GAO/AIMD-99-250 (Washington, D.C.: Sept. 30, 1999).

[33]NGA and NASBO, *The Fiscal Survey of States: June 2010* (Washington, D.C.: June 2010).

[34]NASBO states that total balances include both ending balances and the amounts in states' budget stabilization funds. Total balances reflect the funds that states may use to respond to unanticipated events after budget obligations have been met.

Figure 5: State Government Total Balances as a Percentage of Total Expenditures, State Fiscal Years 1979 to 2010

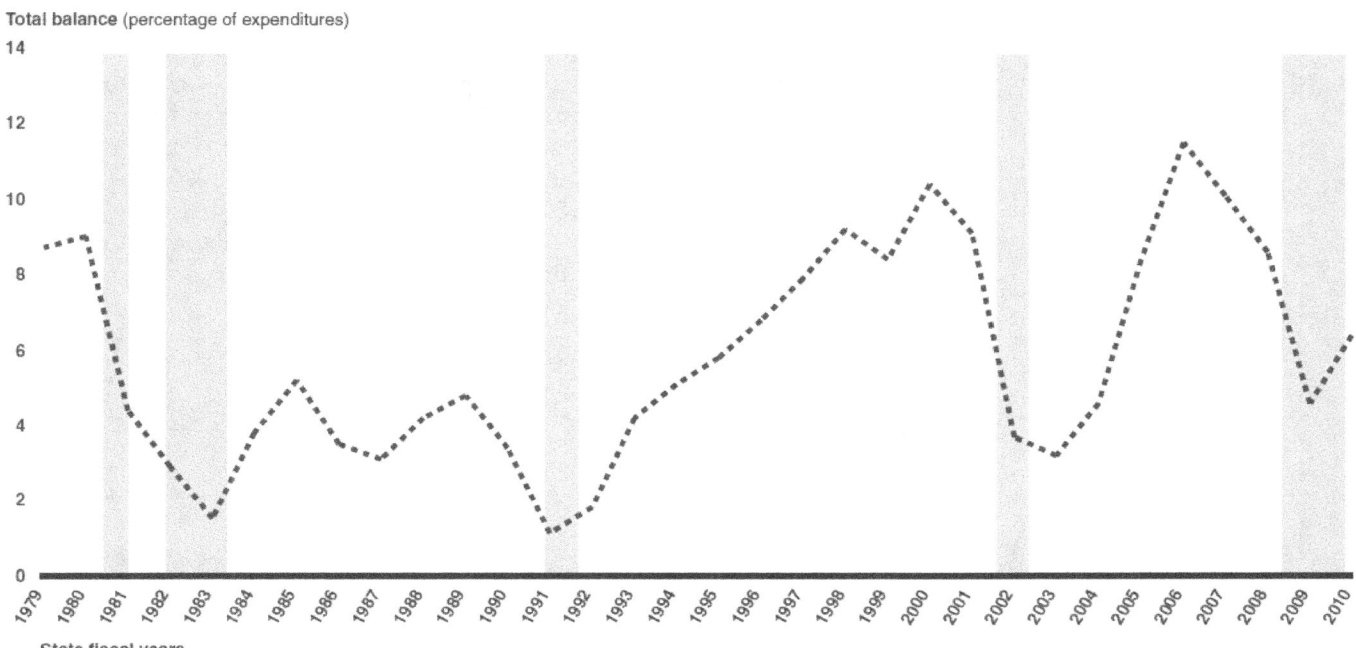

Total balance (percentage of expenditures)

State fiscal years

NBER recessions

∎∎∎∎∎ Total balances

Source: GAO analysis of data from NGA, NASBO, and NBER.

Notes: Total balances are comprised of general fund ending balances and the amounts in state budget stabilization "rainy day" funds. For fiscal year 2010, two states represented $25.4 billion (64 percent) of all states' total balances. Removing these states from fiscal year 2010, states' total balances would be 2.4 percent. Data for state fiscal year 2010 are estimated based on general fund amounts reported by state budget offices. NASBO conducted its 2010 survey from March through May 2010. Reported amounts do not include all states in all years. NBER recession dates are reported in state fiscal years. State fiscal years begin on July 1 of each calendar year for all but four states (Alabama, Michigan, New York, and Texas). For example, we illustrate the national recession beginning July 1990 and ending March 1991 as beginning in the first month of state fiscal year 1991 and ending the ninth month of state fiscal year 1991.

GAO-11-401 State and Local Governments

State and Local Governments also Rely on a Variety of Other Budget Measures to Address Revenue Declines during National Recessions

Since 1973, state and local governments have, in general, borrowed more and saved less during national recessions. Net lending or net borrowing by state and local governments—which is comprised of total receipts minus total expenditures—has fallen after the peak of each business cycle since 1973 (figure 6).[35] While the state and local government sector increased its borrowing substantially during recent recessions, the sector did not increase net investments to the same extent.[36] For example, net borrowing increased from 0.2 percent of GDP in the first quarter of 2006 to 1.15 percent of GDP in the third quarter of 2008 for all state and local governments in the aggregate. In contrast, state and local government investment ranged from 1.1 percent to 1.2 percent of GDP during the same period.

---

[35]In our analysis of state and local government net investment, lending, or borrowing, we used data from BEA's National Income and Product Accounts from the first quarter of 1973 to the first quarter of 2010. Dollar amounts are adjusted for inflation and measured in constant 2009 dollars. Net lending occurs when total receipts exceed total expenditures and net borrowing occurs when total expenditures exceed total receipts. We also analyzed patterns in the difference between current receipts and current expenditures, and obtained similar results. See appendix I for additional information on our methodology.

[36]Net investment is gross government investment minus consumption of fixed capital.

Figure 6: Net Investment, Lending, and Borrowing in the State and Local Government Sector

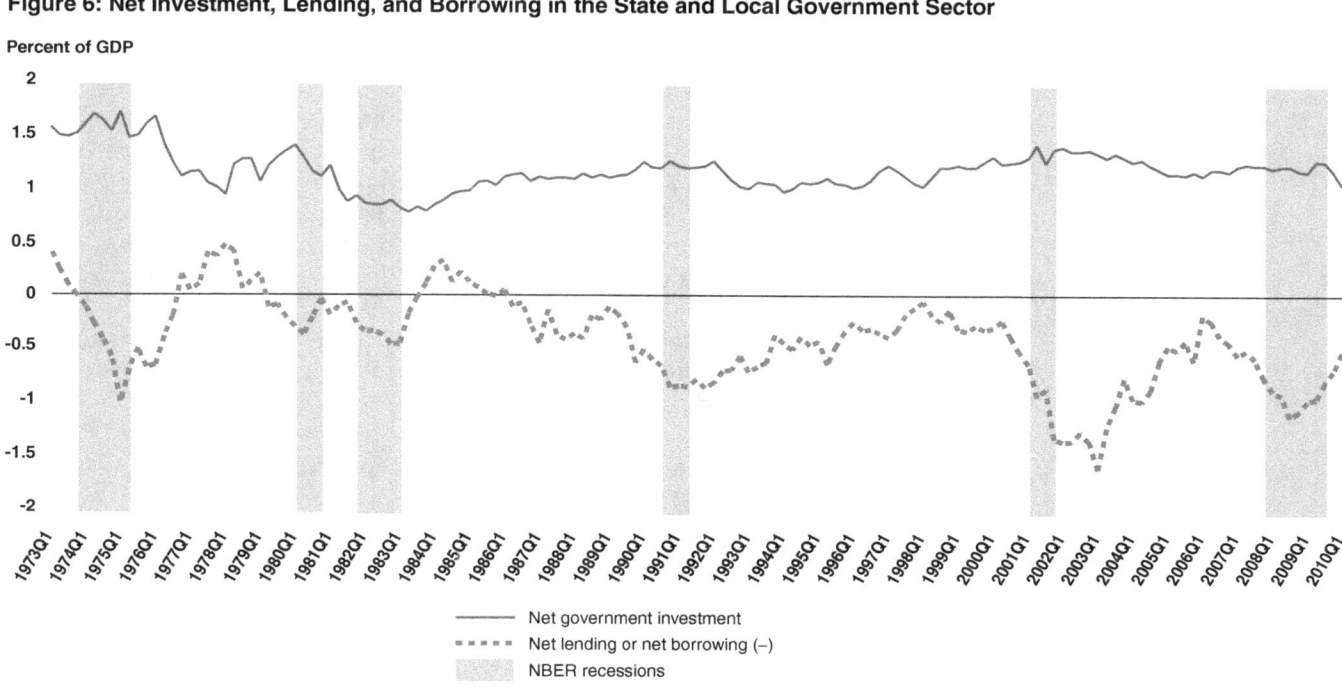

Net government investment

Net lending or net borrowing (–)

NBER recessions

Source: GAO analysis of BEA; NBER data.

Notes: Net lending or net borrowing is comprised of total receipts minus total expenditures. Net lending occurs when total receipts exceed total expenditures and net borrowing occurs when total expenditures exceed total receipts. Net investment is gross government investment minus consumption of fixed capital.

The level of total state and local government debt per capita varies substantially across states.[37] Our analysis found that on average state and local government total debt per capita was $7,695 in fiscal year 2008; however, within individual states debt ranged from a minimum of $3,760 per capita to a maximum of $14,513 per capita. As a percentage of gross state product (GSP), total state and local government debt averaged 16.9 percent and ranged from 6.6 percent to 25.4 percent in fiscal year 2008.[38] State and local government total debt levels appear to correlate with GSP, suggesting that state and local governments within states with more fiscal resources tend to hold more debt.

State budget officials have used other short-term budget measures to address revenue declines while avoiding broad-based tax increases. Some of these strategies include:

- shifting revenues or expenditures across fiscal years,
- securitizing revenue streams,[39]
- reducing payments or revenue sharing to local governments,
- deferring infrastructure maintenance,

---

[37] Our estimates for total debt per capita are derived from U.S. Census Bureau data for states and all local governments within the states' jurisdictions. Projects with longer time frames are typically budgeted separately from the operating budgets and financed by a combination of current receipts, federal grants, and the issuance of debt. About 60 percent of total state and local long-term debt outstanding is in the category of revenue bonds secured by a specific revenue-generating entity and provide no recourse to any other governmental assets or revenues in the event of default. The percentage composition of debt outstanding by type of debt is from U.S. Census Bureau data for fiscal year 2004, the last year in which these data were collected. Some revenue bonds finance public projects including toll roads and water and sewage treatment facilities. Others provide loans for private purposes—the states and localities essentially act as a conduit for reduced-rate financing of private projects and the debt has no claim on state and local revenues and assets. Such private purpose debt has been a fast-growing category over the past 30 years. In contrast to revenue bonds, general obligation bonds, which comprise about 40 percent of total state and local long-term debt outstanding, have payment of principal and interest secured by the full faith and credit of the issuer. Although secured by the full faith and credit of the issuer, general obligation bonds are not necessarily less risky than revenue bonds of the same issuer. Under certain conditions, the bond rating on an issuer's general obligation bonds could be lower than the rating on its revenue bonds.

[38] Gross state product, also known as gross domestic product by state, is the sum of value added from all industries in the state. GDP by state is the state counterpart to the nation's gross domestic product.

[39] For example, some states have securitized revenues from the 1998 Master Settlement Agreement, an agreement between four of the nation's largest tobacco companies to make annual payments to 46 states in perpetuity as reimbursement for past tobacco-related health care costs.

- borrowing from or transferring funds from outside the general fund to address revenue shortfalls, and
- reducing funding levels for pensions.[40]

In addition, a number of state governments have redesigned government programs to improve efficiency and reduce expenditures. According to the National Governor's Association Center for Best Practices (NGA Center), a recession provides state fiscal managers with an opportunity for cutting back inefficient operations.[41] The NGA Center tracked state governments' efforts to restructure government, and in fiscal years 2009 and 2010, a broad range of budget cuts and programmatic changes were enacted in areas such as corrections, K-12 education, higher education, and employee costs (salaries and benefits). While some of these changes were temporary, the NGA Center contends these changes reflect a "new normal" for state government in the long term. The NGA Center found that at least 15 state governments conducted governmentwide reviews to improve efficiency and reduce costs; at least 18 state governments reorganized agencies; and more than 20 state governments altered employee compensation, including enacting pension reforms.

---

[40]Many governments have often contributed less than the amount needed to improve or maintain the funded ratios (actuarial value of assets divided by actuarial accrued liabilities) of their pension plans. Many experts consider a funded ratio of about 80 percent or better to be sound for government pensions. Low funded ratios would eventually require the government employer to improve funding, for example, by reducing benefits or by increasing contributions. See GAO, *State and Local Government Pension Plans: Current Structure and Funded Status*, GAO-08-983T (Washington, D.C.: Jul. 10, 2008) for details.

[41]National Governors Association Center for Best Practices, *Issue Brief: State Government Redesign Efforts 2009 and 2010* (Washington, D.C.: Oct. 18, 2010).

Strategies to Respond to National Recessions Require Decisions on Whether, When, and How to Provide Federal Fiscal Assistance to State and Local Governments

GAO and Other Evaluations of Prior Federal Fiscal Assistance Strategies Identify Design Considerations Including Effective Timing and Targeting of Aid

Evaluations of prior federal fiscal assistance strategies have identified considerations to guide policymakers as they consider the design of future legislative responses to national recessions. To ensure that federal fiscal assistance is effective, we and others have said that policymakers can benefit from considering the following when developing a policy strategy.[42]

- Timing/triggering mechanisms—Fiscal assistance that begins to flow to state and local governments when the national economy is contracting is more likely to help state and local governments avoid actions that exacerbate the economic contraction, such as increasing taxes or cutting expenditures. Since it takes time for state and local government revenues and service demands to return to pre-recession levels, fiscal assistance that continues beyond the end of a recession may help state and local governments avoid similar actions that slow the economic recovery. Federal policy strategies specifically intended to stabilize state and local governments' budgets may have to be timed differently than those designed to stimulate the national economy, because state budget difficulties often persist beyond the end of a recession.

---

[42]For example, see GAO, *Update of State and Local Government Fiscal Pressures*, GAO-09-320R (Washington, D.C.: Jan. 26, 2009); Advisory Commission on Intergovernmental Relations, *Countercyclical Aid and Economic Stabilization* (Washington, D.C.: Dec. 1978); and Douglas W. Elmendorf and Jason Furman, "If, When, How: A Primer on Fiscal Stimulus," *The Hamilton Project Strategy Paper* (Washington, D.C.: Brookings Institution, Jan. 2008).

Securing legislative approval of fiscal assistance through Congress can result in a time lag before such assistance is available. For example, the Recovery Act was passed in February 2009, nearly five quarters after the national recession began in December 2007. There can also be a second lag that results from the time it takes for the federal government to distribute fiscal assistance to the states. Further, state governments often have to set up mechanisms for channeling the funds into the necessary programs. All of this slows the process of spending the money during a recession. In the case of the Jobs and Growth Tax Relief Reconciliation Act of 2003 (JGTRRA), for example, we found that the first federal funds were distributed 19 months after the end of the national recession. A trigger could automatically provide federal assistance, or it could prompt policymakers to take action. Economists at the Federal Reserve Bank of Chicago have described the ideal countercyclical assistance program as one having an automatically activated, pre-arranged triggering mechanism that could remove some of the political considerations from the program's design and eliminate delays inherent to the legislative process. Such a trigger could also specify criteria for ending assistance.

- Targeting—If federal fiscal assistance to state and local governments is targeted based on the magnitude of the recession's effect on each state's economy, this approach can facilitate economic recovery and moderate fiscal distress at the state and local level. Targeting requires careful consideration of the differences in individual states' downturns while also striking a balance with other policy objectives. As discussed below, effective targeting of federal fiscal assistance is dependent upon the selection of indicators that correspond to the specific purpose(s) of the particular policy strategy.

- Temporary—As a general principle, federal fiscal assistance provided in response to national recessions is temporary. While a federal fiscal stimulus strategy can increase economic growth in the short run, such efforts can contribute to the federal budget deficit if allowed to run too long after entering a period of strong recovery. The program can be designed so that the assistance ends or is phased out without causing a major disruption in state government budget planning. If federal assistance is poorly timed, badly targeted, or permanently increases the budget deficit, the short-term benefits of the assistance package may not offset the long-term cost.

- Consistency with other policy objectives—The design of federal fiscal assistance occurs in tandem with consideration of the impact these strategies could have on decision makers' other policy objectives. Such considerations include competing demands for federal resources and an assessment of states' ability to cope with their economic conditions without further federal assistance. As the Peterson-Pew Commission on Budget Reform recently noted in its report, current budget practices recognize the costs of economic emergencies only when these events occur. Although we do not know when recessions will occur or how severe future recessions will be, the current practice of waiting to act until these economic events occur can result in greater public costs than if policy objectives of advance preparation (such as reduced consumption and increased savings during economic upswings) were incorporated into federal fiscal assistance strategies.[43] A standby federal fiscal assistance policy could induce moral hazard by encouraging state or local governments to expect similar federal actions in future crises, thereby weakening their incentives to properly manage risks. For example, states could have less incentive to build, maintain, and grow their rainy day or other reserve funds if they believe they may receive assistance from the federal government during future recessions. Another consideration is the policy objective of maintaining accountability while promoting flexibility in state spending. Past studies have shown that unrestricted federal funds are fungible and can be substituted for state funds, and the uses of such funds can be difficult or impossible to track.[44]

Overall Design Considerations and Policy Goals Influence Selection of Indicators to Time and Target Federal Fiscal Assistance

When policymakers select indicators to time and target federal fiscal assistance in response to a national recession, their selection depends on the specific purposes of the proposed assistance program. For example, during a recession, policymakers may choose to provide general fiscal assistance or assistance for specific purposes such as supporting states' Medicaid or education programs. The indicators chosen to time and target general fiscal assistance could differ from those chosen for the purpose of supporting Medicaid or education. Indicators chosen for Medicaid could also differ from those chosen to provide assistance for education. In addition, different indicators may be needed to determine the timing (triggering on), the targeting (allocating), and the halting (triggering off) of federal fiscal assistance. For example, policymakers could use a national labor market indicator to begin assistance and a state-level indicator to halt assistance. We previously reported on a policy strategy intended to

---

[43]Peterson-Pew Commission on Budget Reform, *Getting Back in the Black* (Nov. 2010).

[44]See GAO, *Temporary State Fiscal Relief*, GAO-04-736R (Washington, D.C.: May 7, 2004).

support state Medicaid programs during economic downturns.[45] This strategy used state unemployment rates to trigger the flow of aid on and off. This strategy used state unemployment rates along with an additional indicator—relative state Medicaid costs—to determine the amount of aid each state receives.

Policymakers could select indicators with the intent of responding to the effects of a particular recession. For example, if policymakers want to begin providing fiscal assistance to state and local governments as states enter an economic downturn, they are challenged by the fact that different states may enter into economic downturns at different times. Policymakers would need to select an indicator that provides information on the overall amount of economic activity in individual states, that is frequent enough to distinguish between different phases of the business cycle, and is available with relatively little lag time.

Timely, state-level, publicly available indicators can be found primarily in labor market data, but are also found in housing market and personal income data.[46] The indicators in table 3 are all commonly used measures of national macroeconomic activity that are also available at the state level. At the national level, indicators such as employment, weekly hours, and housing units authorized by building permits are procyclical, while other indicators, such as unemployment, are countercyclical. The indicators in table 3 are published either monthly or quarterly, and thus cover periods shorter than the length of the typical national recession. These indicators are available with less than a 6-month publication lag, as indicators with publication lags greater than 6 months may not reveal the downturn until it is already over and the recovery has begun.[47]

---

[45]GAO-07-97.

[46]For the purpose of this example, we excluded indicators from private sources because they may not be available in the future and because the methodology used to produce them may be proprietary, making analysis of their reliability difficult. The indicators we list in this report are not an exhaustive list of all indicators available to time and target assistance to states. Depending on the specific policy tool used, policymakers may want to combine the indicators with other information, such as data on increased demand for specific programs, to target assistance for specific programs or state circumstances.

[47]Appendix I provides an additional discussion of our methodology for selecting potential indicators.

Table 3: Selected Indicators for Timing or Targeting Federal Assistance to States

Indicator	Source	Frequency
Coincident index	Federal Reserve Bank of Philadelphia	Monthly
Employment	U.S. Bureau of Labor Statistics (BLS) State and Metro Area Employment, Hours, and Earnings (SAE)	Monthly
	BLS Local Area Unemployment Statistics (LAUS)	Monthly
	BLS Quarterly Census of Employment and Wages (QCEW)	Monthly
Hourly earnings	BLS SAE	Monthly
Housing units authorized by building permits	U.S. Census Bureau	Monthly
Personal income	U.S. Bureau of Economic Analysis (BEA)	Quarterly
Unemployment	BLS LAUS	Monthly
Unemployment rate	BLS LAUS	Monthly
Wages and salaries	BEA	Quarterly
	BLS QCEW	Quarterly
Weekly hours	BLS SAE	Monthly

Source: GAO analysis of BEA, BLS, Federal Reserve Bank of Philadelphia, and U.S. Census Bureau data.

Note: The indicators in this table are not an exhaustive list of all publicly available indicators to time or target assistance to states. Depending on the specific policy strategy used, policymakers may want to combine the indicators with other information, such as data on increased demand for specific programs, to target assistance for specific programs or state circumstances. For example, GAO has reported on a policy strategy that combined information on the change in a state's unemployment rate with an index of the average level of Medicaid expenditures by state.

The illustrative indicators shown in the table above exclude indicators of fiscal stress (such as declines in tax receipts or budget gaps) because they are dependent on state governments' policy choices and because state definitions and measurement techniques vary for calculations such as budget gaps. For example, the list does not include state governments' quarterly tax receipts because this measure reflects policy decisions within each state. Data sources detailing state-level participation in intergovernmental benefit programs are also excluded because program enrollment data can understate the number of individuals eligible for the program. For example, we did not include unemployment insurance claim data from the Employment and Training Administration because BLS has reported that unemployment insurance information cannot be used as a source for complete information on the number of unemployed. We excluded this indicator because claims data may underestimate the number of unemployed because some people are still jobless when their benefits run out, some are not eligible, and some never apply for benefits.

Recent research suggests that some indicators may be better able to trigger assistance on and off than other indicators, depending on the specific purpose of the assistance. Economists from the Federal Reserve Bank of Chicago found that a trigger based on the national aggregate of the Federal Reserve Bank of Philadelphia's State Coincident Indexes—which are comprised of nonfarm payroll employment, average hours worked in manufacturing, the unemployment rate, and wage and salary disbursements—would turn assistance on close to the beginning of a national recession and would turn assistance off close to the end of a national recession.[48] They found that a trigger based on the national unemployment rate also triggered the flow of assistance on close to the beginning of a national recession, but did not trigger the assistance off until well after the national economic recovery was under way, reflecting the lag in employment recovery after recessions. If the goal of aid is to maintain state and local government spending only during the recession, then the State Coincident Indexes may be an appropriate indicator. However, if the goal of aid is to maintain state and local government spending until an individual state's economy fully recovers, the unemployment rate may be an appropriate indicator.

Future Approaches to Federal Fiscal Assistance Can Benefit from Knowledge of Results, Challenges, and Unintended Consequences of Previous Federal Responses

Knowledge of the results, challenges, and unintended consequences of past policy actions can inform deliberations as policymakers determine whether and how to provide federal fiscal assistance in response to future national recessions.[49] Federal responses to prior recessions have included providing various forms of federal fiscal assistance directly to state and local governments as well as decisions not to provide fiscal assistance in response to national recessions. When the federal government has provided fiscal assistance, such assistance has fallen into two general categories: (1) unrestricted or general purpose fiscal assistance,[50] which can include general revenue sharing programs; and (2) federal fiscal assistance through grants for specific purposes. This second category of

---

[48]Richard H. Mattoon, Vanessa Haleco-Meyer, and Taft Foster, "Improving the impact of federal aid to states," *Economic Perspectives* 3Q/2010 (Chicago, Ill.: Federal Reserve Bank of Chicago, 2010), 66-82.

[49]See appendix III for a detailed listing of national recessions since 1973 and examples of federal responses to the question of whether and how to provide fiscal assistance to state and local governments during these periods.

[50]Unrestricted or general-purpose fiscal assistance allows recipients to spend grant funds in the manner they choose with few, if any, federally imposed programmatic or administrative requirements.

assistance has included funding for existing grant programs (including both categorical and formula grants) as well as funding for new grant programs to state and local governments.

Unrestricted or general purpose grants to states and localities maximize spending discretion for state and local governments. This approach has included antirecession payments and general revenue sharing funds to increase state and local expenditures or forestall potential tax increases. Because there are minimal restrictions on the use of these funds, they offer the advantage of not interfering with state spending priorities as well as the opportunity to use the funds quickly. However, our past evaluations, as well as work by others, have noted that this approach also presents challenges and unintended consequences.[51] Due to the nature of such assistance, state and local governments may use unrestricted federal funds for activities that would have otherwise been funded using non-federal sources.[52] Also, in an example from the 1970s, federal antirecession payments were provided through the Antirecession Fiscal Assistance (ARFA) program, which distributed more than $3 billion between July 1976 and September 1978 to state and local governments. State and local governments could use the ARFA funds for the maintenance of basic services customarily provided by these governments, such as public welfare, education and police protection. The ARFA funds were intended to facilitate state spending. However, because the funds were subject to states' standard appropriations procedures, this slowed states' spending of the funds. In its study of ARFA, the Department of the Treasury reported that states appropriated ARFA funds on average 7 months later than the states appropriated their own revenues, thereby delaying entry of the funds into the states' spending stream.[53]

More recently, we found similar issues in our 2004 review of the component of the JGTRRA[54] that provided $10 billion in unrestricted,

---

[51]See, for example, GAO-04-736R; and Congressional Budget Office, *Countercyclical Uses of Federal Grant Programs* (Washington, D.C.: Nov. 27, 1978).

[52]For the most part, the federal grant system does not encourage states to use federal dollars as a supplement rather than a replacement for their own spending, nor is every grant intended to do so. See GAO, *Federal Grants: Design Improvements Could Help Federal Resources Go Further*, GAO/AIMD-97-7 (Washington, D.C.: Dec. 18, 1996).

[53]Office of Revenue Sharing, U.S. Department of the Treasury, *An Analysis of the Antirecession Fiscal Assistance Program (Title II of the Public Works Employment Act of 1976)* (Washington, D.C.: April 1, 1978).

[54]Pub. L. No. 108-27, title IV, 117 Stat. 752 (May 28, 2003).

temporary fiscal relief payments to states that were allocated on a per capita basis.[55] We found that these fiscal relief funds were not targeted to individual states based on the impact of the recession and found it doubtful that these payments were ideally timed to achieve their greatest possible economic stimulus. JGTRRA fiscal relief payments were first distributed to the states in June 2003, about 19 months after the end of the 2001 recession and after the beginning of the economic expansion. However, because employment levels continued to decline even after the economy entered an expansion period, we found that the JGTTRA fiscal relief payments likely helped resolve ongoing state budgetary problems.

Some prior federal fiscal assistance strategies have included use of existing grant programs to deliver assistance to states. This approach has the advantage of targeting funding to reflect federal policy priorities while avoiding the delays involved in establishing and implementing entirely new programs. For example, an amendment to the Comprehensive Employment and Training Act of 1973 (CETA) created Title VI, Emergency Jobs Programs (Title VI), which provided federal fiscal assistance in response to the recession that began in 1973. Title VI adapted the existing CETA federal jobs program to mitigate cyclical unemployment by providing funding to temporarily hire employees in federal, state, and local governments. While policy analysts found that Title VI provided visible and useful services to communities and fiscal relief to some localities, they also found that there were unintended consequences resulting from implementation of the program. According to our prior work, and the work of others, these consequences included the practice by some state governments of laying off current employees and later rehiring the same employees using Title VI funds, instead of using their existing state government funds.[56]

The federal government's responses to the recessions beginning in March 2001 and December 2007 provide recent examples of the use of existing grant structures to expedite the implementation of fiscal assistance. The federal response to both recessions included temporarily increasing the

---

[55]GAO-04-736R.

[56]See GAO, *More Benefits to Jobless Can Be Attained In Public Service Employment*, GAO-HRD-77-53 (Washington, D.C.: Apr. 7, 1977); William Mirengoff and others, *CETA: Accomplishments, Problems, Solutions, A Report*, The Bureau of Social Science Research, Inc. funded by a grant from the Employment and Training Administration, U.S. Department of Labor (Washington, D.C.: 1982).

rate at which states are reimbursed for Medicaid expenditures through an increase to the existing Federal Medical Assistance Percentage (FMAP) formula. Both JGTRRA and the Recovery Act distributed increased FMAP funds to states through the existing Medicaid payment management system. We have reported that increased FMAP funds provided by the Recovery Act were better timed and targeted for state Medicaid needs than funds provided following the 2001 national recession.[57] Overall, the timing of the initial provision of Recovery Act funds responded to state Medicaid needs because assistance began during the 2007 national recession while nearly all states were experiencing Medicaid enrollment increases and revenue decreases. However, state budget officials also referred to the temporary nature of the funds and the fiscal challenges expected to extend beyond the timing of funds provided by the Recovery Act. Officials discussed a desire to avoid what they referred to as the "cliff effect" associated with the dates when the funding ends. The increased FMAP funds provided by the Recovery Act were well targeted for state Medicaid enrollment growth based on changes in state unemployment rates. However, the Recovery Act did not allocate assistance based on state variation in the ability to generate revenue. As a result, the increased FMAP funding did not reflect varying degrees of decreased revenue that states had for maintaining Medicaid service. The increased FMAP funds provided to states following the 2001 recession were provided well after the recession ended and not targeted based on need.

The Recovery Act also increased funding for other existing grant programs to provide fiscal assistance to state and local governments. For example, the Recovery Act provided an additional $2 billion in funds for the Edward Byrne Memorial Justice Assistance Grant (JAG) Program. Consistent with the pre-existing program, states and localities could use their Recovery Act JAG grant funds over a period of 4 years to support a range of activities in seven broad statutorily established program areas including law enforcement, crime prevention, and corrections. In a recent report, we found that of the states we reviewed, all reported using Recovery Act JAG funds to prevent cuts in staff, programs, or essential services. Recipients of Recovery Act JAG funding received their money in one of two ways— either as a direct payment from the Bureau of Justice Assistance or as a pass-through from a state administering agency (SAA)—and they reported

---

[57]See GAO-11-395. The amount of federal funds states receive for their Medicaid programs is determined by the FMAP formula. In response to the 2007 recession, and the recession in 2001, Congress temporarily increased the FMAP to help states maintain their Medicaid programs, as well as provide states with general fiscal relief.

using their funds primarily for law enforcement and corrections. Localities and SAAs that received funds directly from the Department of Justice expended their awards at varying rates, and the expenditure of Recovery Act JAG funds generally lagged behind the funds awarded by the SAAs.[58]

Federal fiscal assistance using existing grant programs can also result in the unintended consequence of hindering the countercyclical intent of the particular assistance program. This can occur because funds flow to states through existing funding formulas typically established for purposes other than providing federal fiscal assistance in response to a national recession. For example, in the case of Medicaid, the regular (base) FMAP formula is based on a 3-year average of a state's per capita income (PCI) relative to U.S. per capita income. PCI does not account for current economic conditions in states, as lags in computing PCI and implementing regular (base) FMAP rates mean that the FMAP rates reflect economic conditions that existed several years earlier.[59] In the case of Recovery Act JAG funding, the Bureau of Justice Assistance allocated Recovery Act JAG funds the same way it allocated non-Recovery Act JAG funds by combining a statutory formula determined by states' populations and violent crime statistics with the statutory minimum allocation to ensure that each state and eligible territory received some funding. This approach offers expedience by relying on the existing formula. However, the purpose of the formula does not take into account states' fiscal circumstances during national recessions.

Prior federal fiscal assistance provided for specific purposes has also included funding for new grant programs. For example, the Recovery Act created a new program, the State Fiscal Stabilization Fund (SFSF), in part

---

[58]GAO, *Recovery Act: Department of Justice Could Better Assess Justice Assistance Program Impact*, GAO-11-87 (Washington, D.C.: Oct. 15, 2010). The Recovery Act JAG Program attempts to meet the overall purposes of the Recovery Act, which include stabilizing state and local government budgets. This report analyzed a nonprobability sample of 14 states.

[59]For a broader discussion, see GAO, *Medicaid Formula: Differences in Funding Ability among States Often Are Widened*, GAO-03-620 (Washington, D.C.: Jul. 10, 2003); and GAO-07-97. The term regular FMAP refers to the base FMAP, as defined under federal law, that is used to determine the percentage of federal assistance for each state's Medicaid service expenditures. The regular FMAP is determined annually by a statutory formula designed to account for income variation across the states. See 42 U.S.C. § 1396d(b). We use the term increased FMAP to refer to temporary FMAP increases above the regular FMAP, as authorized under federal law, that provided states with additional Medicaid funding during national recessions.

to help state and local governments stabilize their budgets by minimizing budgetary cuts in education and other essential government services, such as public safety. SFSF funds for education distributed under the Recovery Act had to first be used to alleviate shortfalls in state support for education to local education agencies and public institutions of higher education. States had to use 81.8 percent of their SFSF formula grant funds to support education and use the remaining 18.2 percent to fund a variety of educational or noneducational entities including state police forces, fire departments, corrections departments, and health care facilities and hospitals. In our prior work, we found budget debates at the state level delayed the initial allocation of education-related funds in some states.[60]

In contrast to these approaches to providing fiscal assistance, in three of the six recessions since 1974, the federal government did not provide fiscal assistance directly to state and local governments (Jan. to July 1980, July 1981 to Nov. 1982, and July 1990 to March 1991).[61] Our prior report has noted that by providing state and local governments with fiscal assistance during downturns, the federal government may risk discouraging states from taking the actions necessary to prepare themselves for the fiscal pressures associated with future recessions.[62] Other analysts have suggested that a recession provides state and local officials with an opportunity for cutting back inefficient operations. If the federal government immediately steps in with fiscal assistance, such an opportunity may be lost.[63] Consequently, policymakers could respond to a future recession by deciding that the federal government should encourage state and local government accountability for their own fiscal circumstances by not providing federal fiscal assistance.

---

[60]GAO, *Recovery Act: One Year Later, States' and Localities' Uses of Funds and Opportunities to Strengthen Accountability*, GAO-10-437 (Washington, D.C.: March 3, 2010).

[61]However, during these recessions, the federal response included increased spending for other programs such as unemployment insurance and increases in existing grants not administered by state and local governments. Federal assistance in response to the recessions beginning in 1973 and 2001 represented a relatively small share of total federal grant funding to the sector. In contrast, the Recovery Act provided a significant increase in grant funding to the sector and helped offset the sector's tax receipt declines.

[62]GAO-04-736R.

[63]Advisory Commission on Intergovernmental Relations, *Countercyclical Aid and Economic Stabilization*, A-69 (Washington D.C.: Dec. 1978).

As a possible alternative to direct federal fiscal assistance to state governments, policy analysts have also considered the concept of a federally sponsored tool to help states prepare for future recessions. We previously discussed proposals for other new programs that would help states respond to recessions but may not provide direct federal fiscal assistance. Examples of these proposed strategies include a national rainy day fund and an intergovernmental loan program that would help states cope with economic downturns by having greater autonomy over their receipt of federal assistance. None of these options have been included in federal fiscal assistance legislation to date.[64]

A national rainy day fund would require individual state governments to pay into a fund that would assist states during economic downturns, while a quasigovernmental agency would administer the fund.[65] The concept of a national rainy day fund is based on establishing a national risk pool to provide countercyclical assistance to states during economic downturns. The national rainy day fund could be modeled on the private unemployment compensation trust fund in that states would be given experience ratings that would require larger contributions based on their individual experience using their own rainy day funds. Proponents of the national rainy day fund argue that it could reduce state governments' fiscal uncertainty by allowing states to use national rainy day funds instead of raising taxes or modifying or cutting programs. An intergovernmental loan program could be an alternative to a national rainy day fund program. The funding for such a loan program could come from either the federal government or from the private capital market, and it could be subsidized and possibly guaranteed by the federal government.

---

[64]See GAO-07-97. We reviewed similar policy strategies in the context of helping states address increased Medicaid expenditures during economic downturns. These proposed strategies include a Medicaid-specific national rainy day fund and intergovernmental loans that would allow states to pool their resources to cope with increased Medicaid costs during economic downturns and could give states greater autonomy over their receipt of federal assistance.

[65]Richard Mattoon, "Creating a National State Rainy Day Fund: A Modest Proposal to Improve Future State Fiscal Performance," *State Tax Notes* (2004): 271-288. The level of aid provided by such a fund could be scaled relative to the severity of the recession in a given state in an effort to address revenue declines related to the business cycle rather than responding to state budget practices or long-term structural declines in states' economies. Many states created their own rainy day or reserve funds in the wake of the 1980-1982 recessions as they were viewed as a good budget practice and were strongly encouraged by debt-rating agencies. States' own rainy day funds are designed to accumulate revenue during periods of strong economic performance with the intent of helping states use them to weather economic downturns.

These alternative strategies to direct federal fiscal assistance to state governments face several design and implementation challenges. Convincing each state to fully fund its required contribution would be an initial challenge to the viability of a national rainy day program. With regard to an intergovernmental loan program, such a program could also delay state governments' budget decisions, as states may need to dedicate portions of future budgets to pay for interest on loans. Determining the appropriate amount of money each state should pay into a national rainy day fund and controlling the risk and cost of any direct intergovernmental loan program would present additional challenges. In addition, representatives from the state organizations and think tanks we spoke with told us they did not see proposals for a national rainy day fund or intergovernmental loan programs as politically feasible. The skepticism regarding these programs included concerns such as accountability issues with a national rainy day program, as well as issues with states' ability to pay back loan interest in a program patterned after the unemployment insurance trust fund.

We are sending copies of this report to interested congressional committees. The report will be available at no charge on GAO's Web site at http://www.gao.gov. If you or your staff have any questions about this letter, please contact Stanley J. Czerwinski at (202) 512-6806 or czerwinskis@gao.gov, or Thomas J. McCool at (202) 512-2700 or mccoolt@gao.gov. Contact points for our Offices of Congressional Relations and Public Affairs may be found on the last page of this report. GAO staff who made major contributions to this report are listed in appendix IV.

Stanley J. Czerwinski
Director, Strategic Issues

Thomas J. McCool
Director, Center for Economics

The Honorable Daniel K. Inouye
Chairman
The Honorable Thad Cochran
Ranking Member
Committee on Appropriations
United States Senate

The Honorable Max Baucus
Chairman
The Honorable Orrin G. Hatch
Ranking Member
Committee on Finance
United States Senate

The Honorable Joseph I. Lieberman
Chairman
The Honorable Susan M. Collins
Ranking Member
Committee on Homeland Security and Governmental Affairs
United States Senate

The Honorable Harold Rogers
Chairman
The Honorable Norman D. Dicks
Ranking Member
Committee on Appropriations
House of Representatives

The Honorable Fred Upton
Chairman
The Honorable Henry A. Waxman
Ranking Member
Committee on Energy and Commerce
House of Representatives

The Honorable Darrell Issa
Chairman
The Honorable Elijah E. Cummings
Ranking Member
Committee on Oversight and Government Reform
House of Representatives

Appendix I: Objectives, Scope, and Methodology

This appendix describes our objectives and the scope and methodology of the work we did to address them, including how we analyzed state and local budgets during national recessions, as well as identified strategies that exist to provide federal fiscal assistance to state and local governments. We also include a list of the organizations we contacted during the course of our work.

Objectives and Scope

The American Reinvestment and Recovery Act of 2009 (Recovery Act) required GAO to evaluate how national economic downturns have affected states over the past several decades.[1] Accordingly, our review focused on the following questions:

- How are state and local government budgets affected during national recessions?
- What strategies exist to provide federal fiscal assistance to state and local governments during national recessions and what indicators can policymakers use to time and target such assistance?

Analyzing How State and Local Government Budgets Are Affected during Recessions

To assess how state and local government revenues and expenditures vary during the business cycle, we analyzed annual data on the following finance variables for the U.S. state and local government sector for 1977-2008: general revenues, own-source revenues, total tax revenues, intergovernmental revenues from the federal government, general expenditures, capital outlays, total current expenditures, current expenditures on elementary and secondary education, current expenditures on higher education, current expenditures on health and hospitals, current expenditures on highways, current expenditures on police and corrections, and current expenditures on public welfare. Detailed definitions of these variables are shown in appendix II. We also analyzed annual data on U.S. Gross Domestic Product (GDP) for 1977-2008. All variables are adjusted for inflation using the GDP deflator and are expressed in constant 2009 dollars. The state and local government finance data are from the U.S. Census Bureau's Annual Survey of State and Local Government Finances and Census of Governments. The GDP and GDP deflator data are from the U.S. Bureau of Economic Analysis's National Income and Product Accounts (BEA NIPA).

---

[1]Pub. L. No. 111-5, Div. B, title V, § 5008, 123 Stat. 115 (Feb. 17, 2009).

To describe the cyclical behavior of state and local government revenues and expenditures, we first plotted the cyclical components[2] of the finance variables and the cyclical component of GDP—our benchmark indicator of the business cycle—to visually examine how they move in relation to one another. We then estimated the correlations of the cyclical components of the finance variables with the cyclical component of GDP for the same year, for 1 to 3 years in the past, and 1 to 3 years in the future. In general, a finance variable is procyclical if the correlation of its cyclical component with the cyclical component of GDP for the same year is positive, and a finance variable is countercyclical if the correlation of its cyclical component with the cyclical component of GDP for the same year is negative. Specifically, we identified a finance variable as procyclical if the correlation was greater than or equal to 0.2 and as countercyclical if the correlation was less than or equal to -0.2. The larger the correlation is in absolute value, the stronger the procyclical or countercyclical relationship. A maximum correlation for, say, the previous year indicates that a finance variable tends to lag the business cycle by 1 year.

We used three alternative methods to estimate the cyclical components of the state and local government finance variables and of GDP: (1) by linearly detrending the natural logarithms of the variables, (2) by using the Baxter-King bandpass filter, and (3) by using the Christiano-Fitzgerald random walk bandpass filter. Figures 7-9 graph the cyclical components of selected finance variables and GDP as estimated by linear detrending. Table 4 shows the correlations we calculated using the cyclical components of the finance variables and GDP as estimated by linear detrending. All three methods produced similar results.

---

[2]We decomposed real state and local government revenues and expenditures and GDP into their (1) long-run trend and (2) business cycle components. The cyclical components of revenues, expenditures, and GDP are the percent deviations in revenues, expenditures, and GDP from their long-run trends.

Figure 7: State and Local Government General Expenditures, GDP, and National Recession Dates, 1977-2008 (Procyclical)

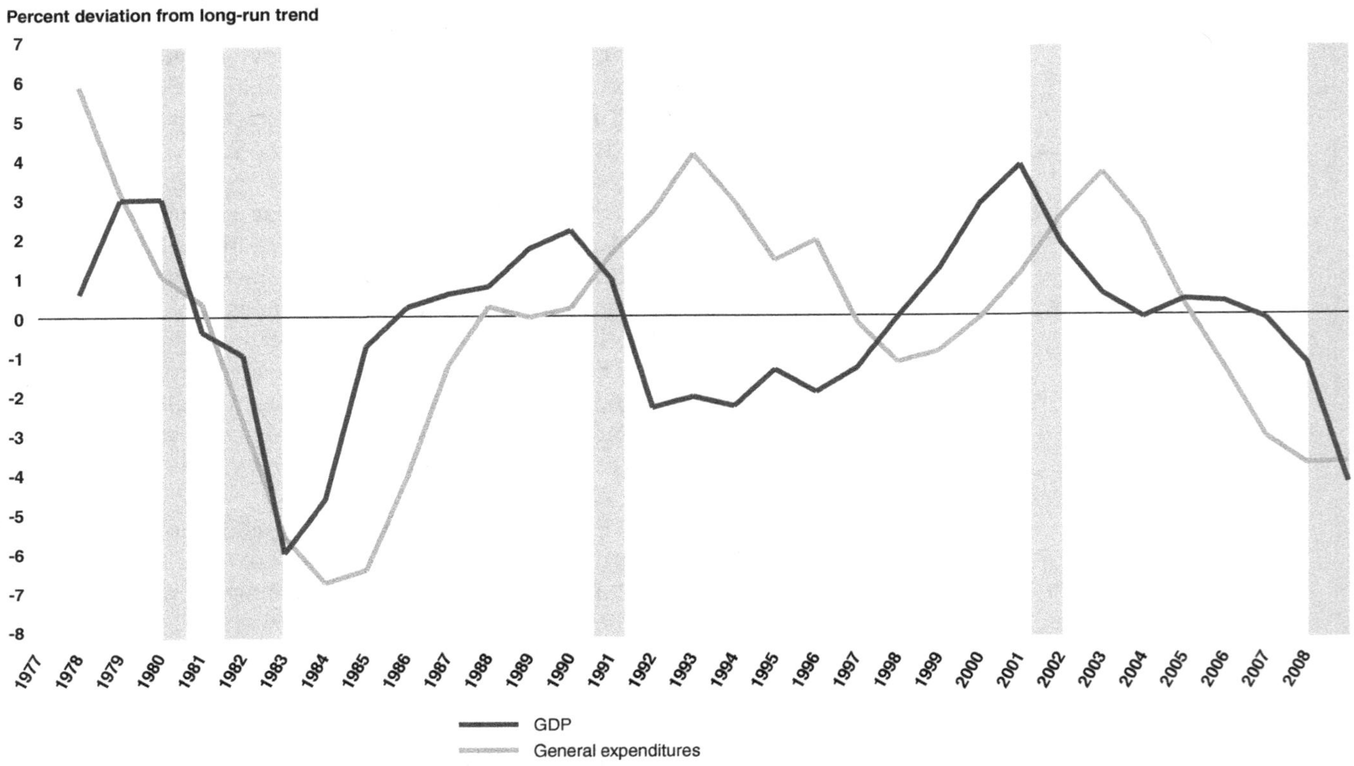

Percent deviation from long-run trend

———— GDP

———— General expenditures

Source: GAO analysis of BEA, U.S. Census Bureau; NBER data.

Note: Shaded areas indicate NBER recession months.

**Figure 8: State and Local Government Current Expenditures on Elementary and Secondary Education, GDP, and National
Recession Dates, 1977-2008 (Procyclical)**

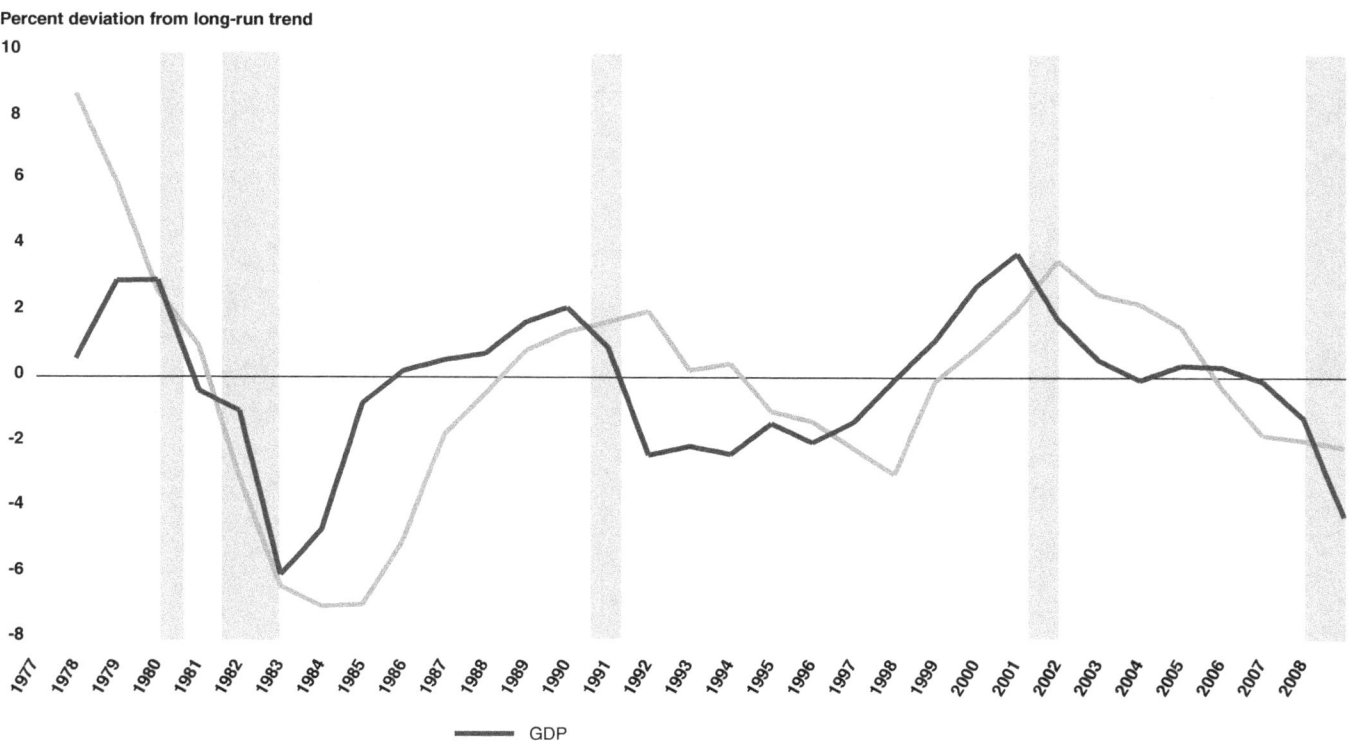

Source: GAO analysis of BEA, U.S. Census Bureau; NBER data.

Note: Shaded areas indicate NBER recession months.

Figure 9: State and Local Government Current Expenditures on Public Welfare, GDP, and National Recession Dates, 1977-2008 (Countercyclical)

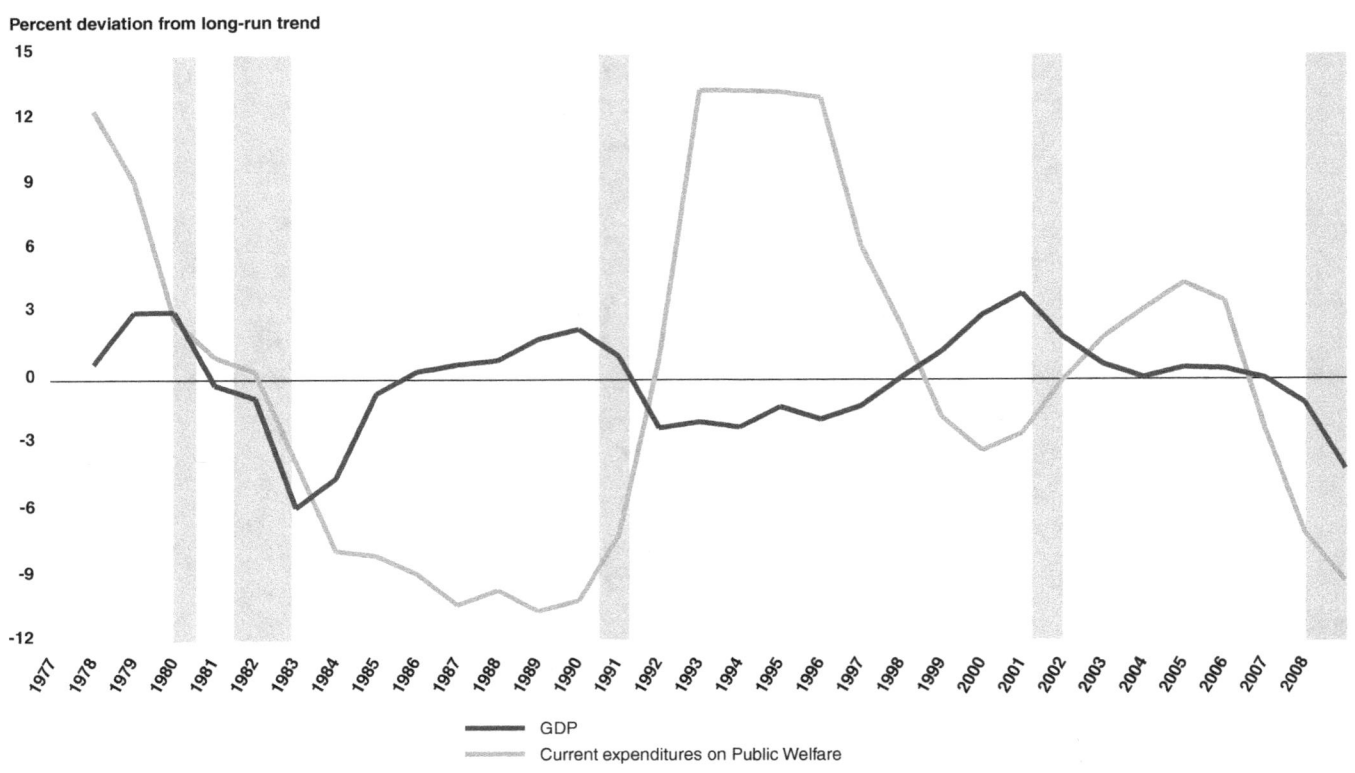

Percent deviation from long-run trend

— GDP

······· Current expenditures on Public Welfare

Source: GAO analysis of BEA, U.S. Census Bureau; NBER data.

Note: Shaded areas indicate NBER recession months.

Table 4: Correlations of the Cyclical Components of State and Local Government Revenues and Expenditures and GDP

	GDP						
	3 years earlier	2 years earlier	1 year earlier	Within the same year	1 year later	2 years later	3 years later
General revenues	-0.29	0.07	0.50	0.62	0.43	0.21	0.09
Own-source revenues	-0.43	-0.13	0.29	0.49	0.44	0.32	0.16
Tax revenues	-0.37	-0.05	0.42	0.64	0.53	0.28	0.05
Intergovernmental revenues from the federal government	0.29	0.27	0.14	-0.03	-0.16	-0.23	-0.11
General expenditures	0.29	0.52	0.53	0.34	0.09	-0.14	-0.25
Current expenditures	0.18	0.31	0.33	0.23	0.09	-0.05	-0.15

	GDP						
	3 years earlier	2 years earlier	1 year earlier	Within the same year	1 year later	2 years later	3 years later
Capital outlays	0.50	0.88	0.86	0.50	0.06	-0.32	-0.40
Current expenditures for elementary and secondary education	0.35	0.67	0.78	0.60	0.29	-0.13	-0.39
Current expenditures for higher education	0.41	0.55	0.53	0.29	0.05	-0.15	-0.27
Current expenditures for health and hospitals	-0.02	-0.14	-0.29	-0.36	-0.27	-0.08	0.08
Current expenditures for highways	-0.08	0.30	0.49	0.53	0.46	0.24	0.06
Current expenditures for police and corrections	-0.12	0.12	0.27	0.38	0.40	0.38	0.27
Current expenditures for public welfare	0.22	0.03	-0.18	-0.31	-0.33	-0.23	-0.08
All other current expenditures	-0.10	0.14	0.33	0.40	0.32	0.19	-0.02

Source: GAO analysis of BEA and U.S. Census Bureau data.

Notes: We used data for the period 1977-2008 for the United States. To describe how state and local government revenues and expenditures change during national economic downturns, we first decomposed real state and local government revenues and expenditures and GDP into their (1) long-run trend and (2) business cycle components. The cyclical components of revenues, expenditures, and GDP are the percent deviations in revenues, expenditures, and GDP from their long-run trends. We then calculated the correlations of the business cycle components of state and local government revenues and expenditures with the business cycle component of GDP. A positive correlation indicates that expenditures are procyclical and a negative correlation indicates that expenditures are countercyclical. Our results may be sensitive to the method we used to estimate the business cycle components of expenditures and of GDP, may not generalize to other time periods, and may not apply to individual U.S. states.

We note several limitations of our analysis. Our results may not generalize to other time periods. Analysis of individual states may produce results that differ from those that we found by analyzing the United States as a whole. Our results may be sensitive to how we aggregated certain state and local finance variables. For example, current expenditures on health and hospitals are the sum of current expenditures on health and current expenditures on hospitals, and these variables may exhibit different behavior when analyzed separately than they do when aggregated. Our results may be sensitive to the methods we used to isolate the cyclical components of the finance variables and GDP. Our results may be sensitive to measurement error we introduced by treating the finance variables as if they were measured on a calendar year basis. In fact, state and local governments keep their financial accounts on a fiscal year basis, and the state and local government finance variables we use are collected so that they cover each government's own fiscal year period, rather than a standard calendar year-based reporting period that cuts across government fiscal years. Specifically, a survey year includes each individual government fiscal year that ended between July 1 of the previous year and June 30 of the survey year. The Census Bureau notes that it uses this methodology because it links directly to the manner in

which governments maintain their financial records. Any attempt to
standardize the time frame for more than 80,000 governments would
create an insurmountable data collection challenge and would be cost
prohibitive.

We analyzed data from BEA NIPA table 3.3 "State and Local Government
Current Receipts and Expenditures" to identify trends in state and local
government tax receipts, net borrowing, investment and savings from 1973
to 2010. We used the GDP price index reported by BEA to deflate values to
2009 dollars. To assess how revenue declines varied between states during
the most recent recession, we calculated year-over-year changes in states'
quarterly tax receipt data from the U.S. Census Bureau. We calculated
variation in state and local government debt per capita across states using
fiscal year 2008 data from the U.S. Census Bureau. Finally, we reviewed
economic and finance literature to better understand how state budgets
are affected during national business cycles.

To estimate the effects of economic downturns on state tax revenues, we
analyzed quarterly data on state tax revenues and wages for the 50 U.S.
states and the District of Columbia for the second quarter of 1992 through
the first quarter of 2010. State tax revenues are from the U.S. Census
Bureau's Quarterly Summary of State and Local Government Tax Revenue.
State wage data are from the U.S. Bureau of Labor Statistics' Quarterly
Census of Employment and Wages. We estimated the elasticity of state tax
revenues with respect to wages—our indicator of the amount of economic
activity in a state. These elasticities are estimates of the percent changes
in state tax revenues that occur when wages in a state increase by 1
percent. We estimated both short-run and long-run elasticities. We used
generalized least squares regressions of the natural logarithm of state tax
revenue on a constant term, quarterly indicators, and the natural logarithm
of wages to obtain the long-run elasticities for each state. We used an error
correction model based on the change in the natural logarithm of state tax
revenues on a constant term, quarterly indicators, the change in the
natural logarithm of wages, and the residual from the long-run regressions
to obtain the short-run elasticities for each state. Table 5 summarizes the
aggregate long-run and short-run elasticities we estimated for each state.
We found that a one percent increase in wages leads, on average, to about
a 1.04 percent increase in state tax revenues in the short run and about a
0.96 percent increase in state tax revenues over the long run.

Table 5: Summary of Elasticities of State Tax Revenues with Respect to Wages

	Average	Minimum	Maximum
Long-run elasticity	0.96	0.16	1.78
Short-run elasticity	1.04	-1.46	2.54

Source: GAO analysis of BEA, BLS, and U.S. Census Bureau data.

Note: Averages are unweighted averages for the 50 U.S. states and the District of Columbia.

To describe state government tax changes and total year-end balances, we collected and analyzed states' general fund data from the National Governors Association (NGA) and National Association of State Budget Officers (NASBO) *The Fiscal Survey of States* (Fiscal Survey) for state fiscal years 1990 to 2010, the dates for which survey data were available on state revenue changes. We used data from the fall publications of the Fiscal Survey because the fall publications provide data on enacted tax changes, as opposed to estimated or proposed tax change data.[3] We report each enacted tax change as a proportion of the total revenue for the fiscal year. Since the Fiscal Survey reports finance data by state fiscal year, we adjusted the National Bureau of Economic Research's (NBER) business cycle peak and trough dates into state fiscal years. According to NASBO, all but four states begin their fiscal years on July 1. We adjusted NBER recession dates in graphics containing Fiscal Survey data in relation to July being the first month of the fiscal year. For example, we illustrate the national recession beginning July 1990 and ending March 1991 as beginning in the first month of state fiscal year 1991 and ending in the ninth month of state fiscal year 1991.

Our analysis of state tax and fee changes and general fund balances is limited by a number of factors. First, we were unable to conduct an analysis of local government tax changes because no comprehensive source for this information exists. Second, NASBO's Fiscal Survey does not include all state revenues and spending. The survey provides aggregate and individual data on states' general fund receipts, expenditures, and balances. NASBO has stated that general funds are the predominant fund for financing a state's services and are the most important elements in determining the fiscal health of states.

---

[3]However, data for state fiscal 2010 are estimated.

Fiscal Survey data are limited in that they are self-reported by state
governments and NASBO does not verify the data by using checks against
supporting documentation. However, NASBO officials provide multiple
opportunities for state budget officials to review data during the survey
period and to discuss data that may be outliers. Also, some states with
biennial budgets do not necessarily isolate the effects of tax changes for
each year, which could skew results. While the Fiscal Survey data have
these limitations, we believe that these data are the best source available
to understand each state's tax policy actions and total balances, and have
found these data to be sufficiently reliable for this purpose.

Identifying Federal Countercyclical Assistance Strategies and Design Considerations

To identify strategies for providing federal assistance to state and local
governments during national recessions, we reviewed federal fiscal
assistance programs enacted since 1973.[4] We identified these programs
and potential considerations for designing a federal assistance program by
reviewing GAO, Congressional Research Service (CRS), and Congressional
Budget Office (CBO) reports and conducting a search for relevant
legislation. The federal fiscal programs we selected to review for this
report were designed to help state governments address the fiscal effects
of national recessions. This legislation was not intended to address long-
term fiscal challenges facing state and local governments. We analyzed the
legislative history and statutory language of past federal assistance
programs, as well as any policy goals articulated in the statutes
themselves. Finally, we interviewed analysts at associations and think
tanks familiar with the design and implementation of federal fiscal
assistance legislation.

To identify factors policymakers should consider when selecting
indicators to time and target federal countercyclical assistance, we
reviewed reports from GAO, CBO, CRS, Federal Reserve Banks, the U.S.
Department of the Treasury (Treasury), and academic institutions. We
considered indicators' availability at the state level and timeliness (in
terms of frequency and publication lag time) to identify indicators
policymakers could potentially use to target and time countercyclical
federal assistance during downturns. We used several decision rules to
assess indicators' availability and timeliness. In terms of availability,
indicators created by private sources were excluded because they may be

---

[4]Although GAO's mandate refers to national economic downturns since 1974, we extended
our review by 1 year to capture the recession that began in November 1973.

available only for a fee, may not produce the data in the future, or their
methodology may be proprietary, making analysis of the data's reliability
difficult. In terms of timeliness, we selected indicators that were published
at least quarterly and with less than a 6-month publication lag. Quarterly
publication ensures the indicator covers time periods that are shorter than
the length of the typical economic downturn, as indicators that cover more
than 3 months may not be able to differentiate between phases of the
business cycle. We selected indicators with a relatively short publication
lag because indicators with publication lags greater than 6 months may not
reveal the downturn until it is already over and the recovery has begun.
For example, we did not include Treasury's total taxable resources—a
measure of states' relative fiscal capacity—as a potential indicator
because it is available on an annual basis with a 3-year lag.

We also excluded indicators that may be influenced by state governments'
policy choices. This includes indicators of fiscal stress, such as declines in
tax receipts or budget gaps. For example, tax receipts reflect states' policy
choices, as states may change tax rates in response to declining revenues
in a recession. We excluded state governments' tax receipts from the table
because this measure is heavily dependent on and reflects policy decisions
within each state. In addition, by choosing an indicator independent of
policy choices, policymakers may reduce the potential for unintended
consequences such as discouraging states from preparing for budgetary
uncertainty (sometimes referred to as moral hazard) when designing a
federal fiscal assistance program.

We also excluded data sources detailing state-level participation in
intergovernmental benefit programs because program enrollment data
may understate the number of individuals eligible for the program. For
example, we did not include unemployment insurance claims data from
the Department of Labor's Employment and Training Administration
because the Bureau of Labor Statistics (BLS) has reported that
unemployment insurance information cannot be used as a source for
complete information on the number of unemployed. This is because
claims data may underestimate the number of the unemployed because
some people are still jobless when their benefits run out, some individuals
are not eligible for unemployment assistance, and some individuals never
apply for benefits.

The indicators discussed in this report are not an exhaustive list of
indicators available to time and target federal fiscal assistance to states.
Depending on the specific policy strategy used, policymakers may want to
combine the indicators with other information, such as data on increased

demand for specific programs, to target assistance for specific programs or state circumstances. For example, GAO has reported on a policy strategy that combined information on the change in a state's unemployment rate with an index of the average level of Medicaid expenditures by state.[5]

We contacted representatives of state and local government organizations and public policy and research organizations to (1) gain insight into public policy strategies and potential indicators for timing and targeting assistance to states; (2) validate our selection of strategies and discuss considerations for designing federal fiscal assistance to state and local governments during national recessions; and (3) obtain views regarding the feasibility and potential effects of these strategies. The organizations we contacted included:

- American Enterprise Institute,
- Center for State & Local Government Excellence
- Center on Budget and Policy Priorities,
- Federal Reserve Bank of Chicago,
- Federal Reserve Bank of St. Louis,
- National Association of State Budget Officers,
- National Governors Association,
- National Conference of State Legislatures,
- National League of Cities
- The Nelson A. Rockefeller Institute of Government, and
- The Pew Center on the States.

We assessed the reliability of the data we used for this review and determined that they were sufficiently reliable for our purposes.

We conducted this performance audit from February 2010 to March 2011, in accordance with generally accepted government auditing standards. Those standards require that we plan and perform the audit to obtain sufficient, appropriate evidence to provide a reasonable basis for our findings and conclusions based on our audit objectives. We believe that the evidence obtained provides a reasonable basis for our findings and conclusions based on our audit objectives.

---

[5]GAO, *Medicaid: Strategies to Help States Address Increased Expenditures during Economic Downturns*, GAO-07-97 (Washington, D.C.: Oct. 18, 2006).

Appendix II: Definitions of Selected Categories of State and Local Government Expenditures and Revenues

This appendix provides summaries of the U.S. Census Bureau's definitions of state and local government revenues and expenditures used in our analyses of how state and local government budgets are affected during national recessions. These summaries are adapted from U.S. Census Bureau, *Government Finance and Employment Classification Manual*, October 2006. We have excluded categories that were not discussed in this report. Employee and retiree health benefits and government pension contributions on behalf of current employees are accounted for in the sector (e.g., education) for which the employees work.

General expenditures—All expenditures except those classified as utility, liquor store, or social insurance trust expenditures.

1. Capital outlays—Direct expenditures for purchase or construction, by contract or government employee, construction of buildings and other improvements; for purchase of land, equipment, and existing structures; and for payments on capital leases.

2. Current expenditures—Direct expenditures for compensation of own officers and employees and for supplies, materials, and contractual services except any amounts for capital outlay (current operations), amounts paid for the use of borrowed money (interest on debt), direct cash assistance to foreign governments, private individuals, and nongovernmental organizations neither in return for goods and services nor in repayment of debt and other claims against the government (assistance and subsidies), and amounts paid to other governments for performance of specific functions or for general financial support (intergovernmental expenditure), including the following categories:

   a. Elementary and secondary education—Current expenditures for the operation, maintenance, and construction of public schools and facilities for elementary and secondary education, vocational-technical education, and other educational institutions except those for higher education; operations by independent governments (school districts) as well as those operated as integral agencies of state, county, municipal, or township governments; and financial support of public elementary and secondary schools.

   b. Health and hospitals—Current expenditures for the provision of services for the conservation and improvement of public health, other than hospital care, and financial support of other governments' health programs; for a government's own hospitals as well as expenditures for the provision of care in other hospitals; for the provision of care in other hospitals and support of other public and private hospitals.

c. Higher education—Current expenditures for higher education activities and facilities that provide supplementary services to students, faculty or staff, and which are self-supported (wholly or largely through charges for services) and operated on a commercial basis (higher education auxiliary enterprises) and for degree-granting institutions operated by state or local governments that provide academic training beyond the high school level, other than for auxiliary enterprises of the state or local institution (other higher education).

d. Highways—Current expenditures for the maintenance, operation, repair, and construction of highways, streets, roads, alleys, sidewalks, bridges, tunnels, ferry boats, viaducts, and related non-toll structures (regular highways) and for highways, roads, bridges, ferries, and tunnels operated on a fee or toll basis (toll highways).

e. Police and corrections—Current expenditures for residential institutions or facilities for the confinement, correction, and rehabilitation of convicted adults, or juveniles adjudicated, delinquent or in need of supervision, and for the detention of adults and juveniles charged with a crime and awaiting trial (correctional institutions); for correctional activities other than federal, state and local residential institutions or facilities (other corrections); and for general police, sheriff, state police, and other governmental departments that preserve law and order, protect persons and property from illegal acts, and work to prevent, control, investigate, and reduce crime (police protection).

f. Public welfare—Current expenditures associated with Supplemental Security Income (SSI), Temporary Assistance for Needy Families (TANF), Medical Assistance Program (Medicaid) (public welfare—federal categorical assistance programs); cash payments made directly to individuals contingent upon their need, other than those under federal categorical assistance programs (public welfare—other cash assistance programs); public welfare payments made directly to private vendors for medical assistance and hospital or health care, including Medicaid (Title XIX), plus mandatory state payments to the federal government to offset costs of prescription drugs under Medicare Part D and payments to vendors or the federal government must be made on behalf of low-income or means-tested beneficiaries, or other medically qualified persons (public welfare—vendor payments for medical care); payments under public welfare programs made directly to private vendors (i.e., individuals or nongovernmental organizations furnishing goods and services) for services and commodities, other than medical, hospital, and health care, on behalf of low-income or other means-tested beneficiaries (public welfare—vendor payments for other purposes); provision, construction, and maintenance of nursing homes and welfare institutions owned and operated by a government for the benefit of needy persons (contingent upon their financial or medical need), and veterans (public welfare—institutions); and all expenditures for welfare activities not classified elsewhere (public welfare—other).

g. Other—Current expenditures for all other functions.

General revenue—General revenue is all revenue except that classified as liquor store, utility, or insurance trust revenue.

1. Intergovernmental revenue from the federal government—Amounts received directly from the federal government. For states, this includes federal grants and aid, payments-in-lieu-of-taxes on federal property, reimbursements for state activities, and revenue received but later transmitted through the state to local governments. For local governments, this category includes only direct aid from the federal government.

2. Own-source revenue—Revenue from compulsory contributions exacted by a government for public purposes, other than for employee and employer assessments and contributions to finance retirement and social insurance trust systems and for special assessments to pay capital improvements (taxes), charges imposed for providing current services or for the sale of products in connection with general government activities (current charges), and all other general revenue of governments from their own sources (miscellaneous general revenue).

Recession period	Countercyclical legislation	Key programs with state needs focus	Description or purpose statement
Nov. 1973 to Mar. 1975	Comprehensive Employment And Training Act of 1973 (CETA), Pub. L. No. 93-203	TITLE II—Public Employment Programs Title VI—Emergency Jobs Programs (Added by Title 1 of Pub. L. No. 93-567)	CETA—Provided job training and employment for economically disadvantaged, unemployed, and underemployed persons through a system of federal, state, and local programs. Titles II and VI—Provided transitional state and local government public service jobs in areas with high unemployment rates.
	Emergency Jobs and Unemployment Assistance Act of 1974, Pub. L. No. 93-567	Title III—Job Opportunities Program	Provided emergency financial assistance to create, maintain or expand jobs in areas suffering from unusually high levels of unemployment.
	Public Works Employment Act of 1976, Pub. L. No. 94-369	Title I—Local Public Works Capital Development and Investment Act of 1976	Authorized funds to establish an antirecessionary program and increased federal funding to states and localities to improve the nation's public infrastructure—roads, bridges, sanitation systems, and other public facilities.
		Title II—Antirecession Fiscal Assistance (ARFA)	ARFA intended to offset certain fiscal actions taken by state governments during recessions, including raising taxes and layoffs. It was designed to achieve three objectives: to maintain public employment, maintain public services, and counter the November 1973—March 1975 recession. Under the ARFA program, state governments received one-third of the allocation, while local governments received two-thirds.
	State and Local Fiscal Assistance Amendments of 1976, Pub. L. No. 94-488		The State and Local Fiscal Assistance Act of 1972 intended to help assure the financial soundness of state and local governments through general revenue sharing. The Amendments of 1976 extended and modified this Act.
	Economic Stimulus Appropriations Act of 1977, Pub. L. No. 95-29	Payments To State And Local Government Fiscal Assistance Trust Fund	For payments to the State and Local Government Fiscal Assistance Trust Fund, as authorized by The State and Local Fiscal Assistance Act of 1972, which was intended to help assure the financial soundness of state and local governments through general revenue sharing.
		Antirecession Financial Assistance Fund	See Antirecession Fiscal Assistance (ARFA) above. An additional amount for ARFA was to remain available until September 30, 1978.
		Employment And Training Assistance	Made economic stimulus appropriations for employment and training.
		Temporary Employment Assistance	Made economic stimulus appropriations for CETA.
		Local Public Works Program	Made economic stimulus appropriations for the fiscal year ending September 30, 1977, as well as for other purposes.

Appendix III: Examples of Congressional
Responses to Assist State and Local
Governments in Response to National
Recessions Since 1973

Recession period	Countercyclical legislation	Key programs with state needs focus	Description or purpose statement
	Public Works Employment Act of 1977, Pub. L. No. 95-28		Increased the authorization for the Local Public Works Capital Development and Investment Act of 1976 (see above) and provided funding for the improvement of public works projects which were to be performed by contracts awarded by competitive bidding.
	Tax Reduction & Simplification Act of 1977, Pub. L. No. 95-30	Title VI—Intergovernmental Antirecession Assistance Act	Authorized additional appropriations to carry out the Anti-Recession Fiscal Assistance program, (see ARFA above) and amended the criterion for determining the state revenue sharing amount and the method of determining the unemployment rate of certain localities.
Jan. 1980 to July 1980	**Did not include federal countercyclical fiscal assistance programs for the purpose of assisting state and local governments.**		
July 1981 to Nov. 1982	**Did not include federal countercyclical fiscal assistance programs for the purpose of assisting state and local governments.**		
July 1990 to Mar. 1991	**Federal countercyclical legislation enacted provided some local support, but programs were not directed at assisting state and local governments.**		
Mar. 2001 to Nov. 2001	Jobs and Growth Tax Relief Reconciliation Act of 2003, (JGTRRA), Pub. L. No. 108-27	Title IV—Temporary State Fiscal Relief, (a) Temporary Increase of the Medicaid Federal Medical Assistance Percentage (FMAP); (b) Assist States in Providing Government Services	Provided (1) fiscal relief through a temporary increase in federal Medicaid funding for all states, as well as (2) general assistance divided among the states for essential government services. The funds were allocated to the states on a per capita basis, adjusted to provide for minimum payment amounts to smaller states.
Dec. 2007 to June 2009	American Recovery and Reinvestment Act of 2009, (Recovery Act) Pub. L. No. 111-5	Division A, Title XIV: State Fiscal Stabilization Fund Division B, Title V: State Fiscal Relief Fund (FMAP)	The purposes of this act include: (1) To preserve and create jobs and promote economic recovery. (2) To assist those most impacted by the recession. (3) To provide investments needed to increase economic efficiency by spurring technological advances in science and health. (4) To invest in transportation, environmental protection, and other infrastructure that will provide long-term economic benefits. (5) To stabilize state and local government budgets, in order to minimize and avoid reductions in essential services and counterproductive state and local tax increases.
	Education Jobs and Recovery Act FMAP Extension, Pub. L. No. 111-226 (federal legislation enacted on August 10, 2010, to amend the Recovery Act.)	Title I: Education Jobs Funds	Funds awarded to local educational agencies under this law may be used only to retain existing employees, to recall or rehire former employees, and to hire new employees, in order to provide educational and related services. These funds may not be used to supplement a rainy-day fund or reduce debt obligations incurred by the state.

Appendix III: Examples of Congressional
Responses to Assist State and Local
Governments in Response to National
Recessions Since 1973

Recession period	Countercyclical legislation	Key programs with state needs focus	Description or purpose statement
		Title II: State Fiscal Relief and Other Provisions, Extension Of Recovery Act Increase In FMAP	Provided for an extension of increased FMAP funding through June 30, 2011, but at a lower level.

Source: GAO analysis of federal fiscal assistance public laws and pertinent legislative history.

Appendix IV: GAO Contacts and Staff Acknowledgments

GAO Contacts	Stanley J. Czerwinski, Director, Strategic Issues, (202) 512-6806 or czerwinskis@gao.gov. Thomas J. McCool, Director, Center for Economics, (202) 512-2700 or mccoolt@gao.gov.
Staff Acknowledgments	Michelle Sager (Assistant Director), Shannon Finnegan (Analyst-in-Charge), Benjamin Bolitzer, Anthony Bova, Amy Bowser, Andrew Ching, Robert Dinkelmeyer, Gregory Dybalski, Robert Gebhart, Courtney LaFountain, Alicia Loucks, Donna Miller, Max Sawicky, and Michael Springer also made key contributions to this report.

Related GAO Products

Medicaid: Improving Responsiveness of Federal Assistance to States During Economic Downturns. GAO-11-395. Washington, D.C.: March 31, 2011.

Recovery Act: Opportunities to Improve Management and Strengthen Accountability over States' and Localities' Uses of Funds. GAO-10-999. Washington, D.C.: September 20, 2010.

State and Local Governments: Fiscal Pressures Could Have Implications for Future Delivery of Intergovernmental Programs. GAO-10-899. Washington, D.C.: July 30, 2010.

Recovery Act: States' and Localities' Uses of Funds and Actions Needed to Address Implementation Challenges and Bolster Accountability. GAO-10-604. Washington, D.C.: May 26, 2010.

Recovery Act: One Year Later, States' and Localities' Uses of Funds and Opportunities to Strengthen Accountability. GAO-10-437. Washington, D.C.: March 3, 2010.

State and Local Governments' Fiscal Outlook: March 2010 Update. GAO-10-358. Washington, D.C.: March 2, 2010.

Recovery Act: Status of States' and Localities' Use of Funds and Efforts to Ensure Accountability. GAO-10-231. Washington, D.C.: December 10, 2009.

Recovery Act: Recipient Reported Jobs Data Provide Some Insight into Use of Recovery Act Funding, but Data Quality and Reporting Issues Need Attention. GAO-10-223. Washington, D.C.: November 19, 2009.

Recovery Act: Funds Continue to Provide Fiscal Relief to States and Localities, While Accountability and Reporting Challenges Need to Be Fully Addressed. GAO-09-1016. Washington, D.C.: September 23, 2009.

Recovery Act: States' and Localities' Current and Planned Uses of Funds While Facing Fiscal Stresses. GAO-09-829. Washington, D.C.: July 8, 2009.

Recovery Act: As Initial Implementation Unfolds in States and Localities, Continued Attention to Accountability Issues Is Essential. GAO-09-580. Washington, D.C.: April 23, 2009.

American Recovery and Reinvestment Act: GAO's Role in Helping to Ensure Accountability and Transparency. GAO-09-453T. Washington, D.C.: March 5, 2009.

Update of State and Local Government Fiscal Pressures. GAO-09-320R.Washington, D.C.: January 26, 2009.

State and Local Fiscal Challenges: Rising Health Care Costs Drive Long-term and Immediate Pressure. GAO-09-210T. Washington, D.C.: November 19, 2008.

Medicaid: Strategies to Help States Address Increased Expenditures during Economic Downturns. GAO-07-97. Washington, D.C.: October 18, 2006.

Federal Assistance: Temporary State Fiscal Relief. GAO-04-736R. Washington, D.C.: May 7, 2004.

GAO's Mission	The Government Accountability Office, the audit, evaluation, and investigative arm of Congress, exists to support Congress in meeting its constitutional responsibilities and to help improve the performance and accountability of the federal government for the American people. GAO examines the use of public funds; evaluates federal programs and policies; and provides analyses, recommendations, and other assistance to help Congress make informed oversight, policy, and funding decisions. GAO's commitment to good government is reflected in its core values of accountability, integrity, and reliability.
Obtaining Copies of GAO Reports and Testimony	The fastest and easiest way to obtain copies of GAO documents at no cost is through GAO's Web site (www.gao.gov). Each weekday afternoon, GAO posts on its Web site newly released reports, testimony, and correspondence. To have GAO e-mail you a list of newly posted products, go to www.gao.gov and select "E-mail Updates."
Order by Phone	The price of each GAO publication reflects GAO's actual cost of production and distribution and depends on the number of pages in the publication and whether the publication is printed in color or black and white. Pricing and ordering information is posted on GAO's Web site, http://www.gao.gov/ordering.htm. Place orders by calling (202) 512-6000, toll free (866) 801-7077, or TDD (202) 512-2537. Orders may be paid for using American Express, Discover Card, MasterCard, Visa, check, or money order. Call for additional information.
To Report Fraud, Waste, and Abuse in Federal Programs	Contact: Web site: www.gao.gov/fraudnet/fraudnet.htm E-mail: fraudnet@gao.gov Automated answering system: (800) 424-5454 or (202) 512-7470
Congressional Relations	Ralph Dawn, Managing Director, dawnr@gao.gov, (202) 512-4400 U.S. Government Accountability Office, 441 G Street NW, Room 7125 Washington, DC 20548
Public Affairs	Chuck Young, Managing Director, youngc1@gao.gov, (202) 512-4800 U.S. Government Accountability Office, 441 G Street NW, Room 7149 Washington, DC 20548